THE
WISE USE
AGENDA

THE CITIZEN'S POLICY GUIDE TO ENVIRONMENTAL RESOURCE ISSUES

THE WISE USE AGENDA

A Task Force Report Sponsored by the Wise Use Movement

Edited by Alan M. Gottlieb

Introduction by Ron Arnold

THE FREE ENTERPRISE PRESS
BELLEVUE

FIRST EDITION
Published by The Free Enterprise Press

Typeset in New Century Schoolbook on Iconix computers by The Free Enterprise Press, Bellevue, Washington.

The Free Enterprise Press is a division of the Center for the Defense of Free Enterprise, 12500 N.E. Tenth Place, Bellevue, Washington, 98005. Telephone 206-455-5038.

This book is distributed by Merril Press, P.O. Box 1682, Bellevue, Washington, 98009. Additional copies may be ordered from Merril Press at $9.95 each. Telephone 206-454-7008.

LIBRARY OF CONGRESS CATALOGING-IN-PUBLICATION DATA

The Wise use agenda.

     Result of Multiple Use Strategy Conference, held Aug. 1988 in Reno, Nev.; sponsored by the Center for the Defense of Free Enterprise.
     Bibliography: p.
     1. Environmental policy--United States. 2. Environmental protection--United States. I. Gottlieb, Alan M. II. Multiple Use Strategy Conference (1988 : Reno, Nev.) III. Center for the Defense of Free Enterprise. IV. Title: Citizen's policy guide to environmental resource issues.
HC110.E5W57 1989   363.7'00983   89-1595
ISBN 0-939571-05-4

PRINTED IN THE UNITED STATES OF AMERICA

Contents

Introduction

THIS AGENDA CAME INTO BEING as the result of a conference. A national conference was held in August of 1988 to bring together many like-minded citzens concerned about the environment and human development. It was sponsored by the Center for the Defense of Free Enterprise and christened the Multiple Use Strategy Conference. The nearly 300 attendees, all leaders in natural resource use fields, came from all over the United States and Canada to the meeting site in Reno, Nevada.

Four distinct constituencies attended: Most conference invitees were executives of public interest membership organizations dealing in some way with environmental or resource issues. The next largest group was unaffiliated but interested individuals who shared the common passion for life on this planet. The third consisted of trade group and government representatives, while the smallest representations came from industrial firms focused around natural resource extraction and conversion: mining, fisheries, timber, petroleum, agriculture. They examined and debated the major economic/ecologic issues facing the world today:

Will man inevitably destroy the ecosystem of the Earth he depends upon?

Is human development inherently harmful to the natural environment?

Are there ways to develop natural resources for human use with minimal disruption to nature?

Can humanity live in productive harmony with the earth?

Is today's environmental movement over-reacting to environmental problems and giving too little attention to environmental solutions?

Are we threatening mankind's econosystem with needless restrictions on human use of the Earth's ecosystem?

What is the proper place of mankind and industrial civilization in the natural world?

The Multiple Use Strategy Conference not only yielded provocative and innovative answers to these questions, it also provided the laboratory for a major social development: That its disparate and dispersed individual members had for the past few years been unwittingly preparing the way for a new movement of societal change. The Farm Bureau Federation had for years been working toward wise use unaware of its natural ally, the National Council for Environmental Balance; Oregonians for Food and Shelter had little awareness of the National Inholders Association (private property owners located within governmental boundaries). The National Rifle Association had studied the impacts of Wilderness designation on hunting, but had only recently learned of a group with parallel interests, the Wilderness Impact Research Foundation. And so forth. Once the 250 conference participants met in the same room -- most of whom had never even heard of each other before -- they found that their various organizations had one thing in common: advocacy for the wise use of resources. And they discovered that between them their organizations represented a total membership in excess of ten million people.

They were not single-minded preservationists and they were not single-minded apologists for industrial development. They were representatives of a new balance, of a middle way between extreme environmentalism and extreme industrialism. They were looking for genuine solutions to the age-old problem of getting a living from the Earth without terminally fouling our own nest -- or that of our fellow creatures. They felt that industrial development can be directed in ways that enhance the Earth, not destroy it. And that meant that industry was a positive value in man's history, that industry was something that needs to be protected and fostered in the same way and for the same reasons that nature must be protected and fostered: there are those who would thoughtlessly harm the very source of our well-being.

Thus, for the first time, industry had a core of citizen supporters with a clear-eyed critical understanding of the problems of industry. They were a social force that has been growing for more than a decade without even being aware of its own existence. They were the founders of the Wise Use Movement.

By the end of the three-day conference, the participants had decided that they must take decisive action. They formally recognized that they were indeed a movement and accepted the concomitant responsibilities, the first of which was to set an agenda for the wise use of the environment and present it to the incoming Administration. The Conference thus mandated that the Center for the Defense of Free Enterprise gather statements and recommendations from all attendees and edit them into a coherent document.

This book is the result of that labor. The Wise Use Agenda is a new view and a new hope for man and nature alike. It refuses to accept the defeatist notion that man will inevitably destroy his own home. It refuses to accept the blind optimism of the engineer who trusts only in rational thought and neglects humanity's rich emotional archetypes. It recognizes the need for a new outlook, a new holistic way of understanding man and nature that does not promote extremism in either unbridled development or fanatic preservationism. It strives to discover workable methods to achieve sustainable development: enough food, clothing, shelter and jobs for all mankind to live in humane conditions while enhancing the natural environment through thoughtful and knowledgable design.

The new movement's Neo-Environmental philosophy adds depth and character to both the "business-as-usual" outlook of industry and the "only nature is pure" outlook of contemporary environmentalism. The New Environmentalism is a bridge, a connecting point, between categories that have remained sadly apart in American thought. It bodes well for a future population that respects the Earth while using it efficiently.

The members of the Wise Use Movement have no glowing illusions about how difficult their ideal may be to achieve. But they have the strongest belief that their ideal is the right one for the future, that they represent the shape of environmentalism in the 21st Century.

In reviewing the many submissions to this Agenda, the most striking feature of Wise Use Movement thought is the care devoted to explaining the movement's basic outlook to those who may not be familiar with today's complex and highly technical resource issues. While helping editor Alan M. Gottlieb sort the voluminous materials, I culled a selection of pithy phrases that communicate in a few words what many pages could not. I call such an epigram a "Wise Use Motto." Here are a few I found memorable:

Man and Nature Together: A World That's Whole

Use It Wisely So Your Grandkids Can

Wise Use Is Being A Good Citizen Of The Universe

Wise Use: Nature For People - People For Nature

Just Because It's Human, Don't Knock It -
You May Be Human Yourself Some Day

Our Goal Is Productive Harmony

Pollution Is Not, As We Are So Often Told, A
Product Of Moral Turpitude. It Is An Inevitable
Consequence
Of Life At Work. We Should Put Our Waste
To Good Use, Not Ban It.

Diamonds, Ha! *Sustainable Development* Is Forever

The Earth Is Tougher Than You Think
So Don't Tempt It To Beat Your Brains Out

The Basic Law of Toxicology Is: The Dose Is The
Poison; e.g. Everything Is Toxic
In A Large Enough Dose.
So If You Want Zero Risk, You'll Just Have To
Ban The Entire Cosmos.

Love All Of Nature,
Not Nature Apart
From The Oh-So-Human Soul That Loves It

On The Greenhouse Effect:
Better To Plant An Oxygen-Giving Tree
Than Curse The Carbon Dioxide

Wise Use Isn't Like
Having Your Cake And Eating It Too:
It's Like Finding Novel Ways To Get More Cake
By Taking Advantage Of Used Cake

You Can't Take Pictures Of The Forest
Without Cutting Some Of The Trees Down:
What Do You Think They Make Film Out Of?

You Have A Right To Be Here,
No Less Than The Trees And The Stars

Don't Be Stingy - Share The Earth

Admittedly, some of these mottos, such as the old chestnut from *Desiderata,* are little more than clichés or bumper sticker philosophizing. Yet they can't be dismissed so lightly. I was impressed by the urge of Wise Use advocates to get their message across in terms the average person can understand *as well as in the technical language of their formal recommendations.* The Wise Use Movement is not an exclusive club, it is a broad-based movement seeking to gain a broader base. It has been gestating for more than a decade. In this agenda it has been born.

Ron Arnold
Editor In Chief
Free Enterprise Press

Acknowledgments

THOSE WHO CONTRIBUTED recommendations for this agenda are listed in Section II as signatories of letters to President Bush. We deeply appreciate the thought and effort that went into these detailed, practical recommendations.

Funding was provided in part by a grant from the Center for the Defense of Free Enterprise. Additional funds or in-kind services were provided by other Wise Use Movement citizen activist organizations. These include the Alliance for Environment and Resources, Sacramento, California; Modoc Cares, California, the National Reversionary Property Rights Owners Association, American Freedom Coalition, and the National Inholders Association.

Foundation grants were received from the F. M. Kirby Foundation and from the many foundations which have traditionally supported the Center for the Defense of Free Enterprise. The Five County Association of Governments representing Beaver, Garfield, Iron, Kane and Washington Counties of Utah provided a special grant for publication of the agenda.

Funding for printing and distribution of *The Wise Use Agenda* was provided by a task force led by Arnold Ewing of Seneca Sawmills, Eugene, Oregon. Generous grants were received from Fibreboard, Sun Studs, Inc., R. B. Cone, Burkland Lumber Company, Vernon R. Morgan, L. Sterling Hanel, Robert G. Scott, along with many others.

We especially appreciate the advice and consultation of numerous scholars and technical experts during the editing of the submissions. Dr. Irwin Tucker of the National Council for Environmental Balance provided valuable insights into many scientific debates and helped to formulate a number of submissions. Jim Petersen, public affairs consultant, offered many useful suggestions. Ron Arnold, editor in chief of the Free Enterprise Press performed the mechanical editing tasks and supervised the production of the book.

Preface:
A Call to Action

NATURAL RESOURCE ISSUES are among the most complex and emotional problems facing mankind today. Our leading magazines routinely feature front covers depicting *the endangered earth*. In fright and alarm we ask ourselves first, "What are we doing wrong?" Then we begin to ask, "What's wrong with us?" As we cast about seeking to place blame for misusing the earth, our first impulse is to *stop using the earth*. But we cannot stop using the earth. It is as suicidal to strangle our economy in a fit of guilt and alarm as it would be to willfully continue misusing the earth. Particularly in the midst of today's crisis atmosphere, we must find ways to use the earth wisely and find ways to understand that *the earth can be used wisely*. It is not enough to develop environmentally sound technology, we must also develop the public will to use sound technology without a reactionary backlash against all technology. We need an environmental policy that protects both ecology and economy. That is the mission of this agenda: To point toward lifestyles and mindstyles of productive harmony with nature.

But even though commentators have pointed out again and again that man is an integral component of the earth's ecosystem, an ill-conceived strain of purism has polluted the public debate with a fanatic anti-people ideology. There is little tolerance for humanity and our mistakes in modern environmentalist thought. Man's actions tend to be seen only as a threat to the Earth's welfare. The attitude behind much environmentalist legislation is that man has no right to be here and our inquisitive and inventive mind has no place in nature as nature "ought to be." We even read of experts warning that human intelligence itself is an unnatural development that poses only grave danger to the Earth and could have no possible benefit to anything -- not to us, not to other species.

The Wise Use Movement argues that such dour anti-people attitudes have no place in an ethical view of mankind. We have a right to be here. We are as natural as the whales. Our curiosity and intelligence have a rightful place in nature (or we wouldn't have it: Nature is unforgiving of serious mistakes). Our mistakes are no more stupid than those of other creatures such as the elephant that eats itself out of its own habitat -- and elephants cannot solve their self-made dilemmas, but people can. As I said, anti-people attitudes have no place in an ethical view of mankind. And they certainly have no place in the legislative structure of American law.

Yet during the past twenty years that disdainful "people are no damn good" attitude has come to pervade American law in one environmental statute after another. The cure is often worse than the disease. Coal-fired generators are required to use a specific type of scrubber to eliminate sulfur emissions according to a Clean Air Act amendment. However, the law did not take into consideration Western coal deposits that contain little natural sulfur. Power plants using this Western coal discovered that their expensive scrubbers would not activate at all without a certain minimal sulfur content in the coal, so the power companies had to buy sulfur and add it to their clean coal in order to make the scrubbers work so they could clean the sulfur for coal that didn't have enough. It makes wonderful sense if your only intention is to punish industry for having made mistakes. But to the average citizen it is an outrageous and costly example of bureaucratic stupidity.

Unfortuantely, few environmental laws on the books today are lacking in all manner of such ill-considered demands and requirements which end up misusing valuable resources in projects that do not achieve the environmental goal of the law. We have more than twenty years worth of "command and control," "do it this way or else" legislation enshrined in court test case decisions that uphold these stupidities. The result is a gigantic morass of regulations that virtually stifle human intellectual and economic progress while doing little to solve actual environmental problems. The sad part is that our present environmental problems could be dealt with successfully if only the laws were redesigned to correct the problem rather than punish mistakes or merely study the problem to death -- "paralysis by analysis."

The Wise Use Agenda is a first bold step in that direction: to redesign American law, court cases, and public attitudes that contribute to the problem. The message of the Wise Use Agenda is straightforward: We can do it right. We can live in productive harmony with nature. We will inevitably make mistakes, but we have the ability and the good will to correct and ultimately avoid those mistakes.

But the Wise Use Movement can't do it alone. Its vision for correcting misunderstanding about resources as contained in this Agenda must spread to every newspaper and television screen in the nation. Examples of success must be shown alongside the mistakes. The public must come to know the whole story of man and the environment, not just the doom and gloom. Disasters sell newspapers, we know. But a steady diet of nothing but media disaster-mongering in the midst of genuine harmonious progress will sell more than newspapers: It will sell the industrial might and the brain power of America down the river into oblivion. The Wise Use Agenda, spread to the widest possible readership and heeded by our national leaders, will go a long way toward correcting the problems of both the environment and overzealous environmentalism. Wise Use will *be* the environmentalism of the 21st Century.

Alan M. Gottlieb

Letter of Transmittal
to President George Bush

President George Bush
The White House
Washington, D.C.

Mr. President:

We, the citizen members of the Wise Use Movement, offer for the consideration of your Administration the following recommendations affecting man and nature, ecology and economy, in the hope that together we can solve the serious economic and environmental problems facing our nation.

This agenda seeks to identify and promote those policies and technologies that will yield the greatest good for the greatest number over the long run by working in productive harmony with nature and preventing environmental damage.

In order to make our recommendations clear to the general public despite their technical nature, we have divided this agenda into three sections:
    1. This cover letter;
    2. The top twenty-five goals;
    3. Letters to you from the Wise Use Movement. These letters were gathered from the groups that provided the recommendations that were edited into the top twenty-five goals.

1

This document is unique in American history: A genuine grass roots voice asking that we use our environment wisely, that we seek a middle ground, that we follow the ideal of sustainable development, that we go to neither extreme of reckless plunder of the Earth or blind opposition to progress.

The Wise Use Agenda for the Environment affects these seven executive agencies:

Forest Service
National Park Service
Bureau of Land Management
Fish and Wildlife Service
Office of Management and Budget
Council on Environmental Quality
Environmental Protection Agency

THE WISE USE AGENDA addresses these resource issues:

Transportation	Minerals Policy	Clean Air
Clean Water	Grazing Policy	Privatization
Energy	Wise Pesticide Use	Recreation
	Wilderness Impact	

Toxic Materials Policy	Global Wise Use
Wise Use Education	Paying for Scenery
Wild and Scenic Rivers	Property Rights
Obstructionism Liability	Community Stability
Critical Eco/Econosystems	Third World Wise Use
Endangered Species Impact	Municipal Code Abuse
General Condemnation Act	Declaration of Taking Act

National Industrial Policy Act
Private Rights in Federal Lands
National Commodity Production Systems

THE WISE USE AGENDA proposes these broad policy goals for America:

1. Adopt policies that will promote both the use of the environment and wisdom in that use: Adequate natural resources for our social and economic well-being developed by means that protect the natural environment.

2. Identify and encourage wise use technologies that work in productive harmony with nature.

3. Promote public awareness of outstanding examples of man working in harmony with nature.

4. Discourage extremism in both resource use and protection. National policy should officially recognize that human economic development can be carried out by means that enhance the natural environment.

5. Administer wise use policy with equal sensitivity toward natural values and human values.

We appreciate this opportunity to present the Wise Use Agenda to the Bush Administration and to the people of America.

-- The Wise Use Movement

SECTION I
THE TOP
TWENTY-FIVE GOALS

1. Initiation of a Wise Use Public Education Project by the U.S. Forest Service explaining the wise commodity use of the national forests and all federal resource lands. An important message is that the federal deficit can be reduced through prudent development of federal lands. A public outreach action plan and implementation shall be accomplished using print and electronic media to reach the broadest possible public with the commodity use story of the National Forest System.

2. Immediate wise development of the petroleum resources of the Arctic National Wildlife Refuge (ANWR) in Alaska as a model project showing careful development with full protection of environmental values.

3. The Inholder Protection Act. To provide congressional recognition to the lawful status as property owners of inholders within all federal areas.

5

The United States shall irrevocably recuse itself from all eminent domain power over inholdings. The Act should repeal the General Condemnation Act of 1888 and the Declaration of Taking Act of 1933.   Acquisition of private land from federal inholders shall henceforth take place only with the un-coerced agreement of the inholder.

4. Passage of the Global Warming Prevention Act to convert in a systematic manner all decaying and oxygen-using forest growth on the National Forests into young stands of oxygen-producing, carbon dioxide-absorbing trees to help ameliorate the rate of global warming and prevent the greenhouse effect.   The federal government shall also help fund and coordinate urban tree planting on all federal property as part of this critical program.

5. Creation of the Tongass National Forest Timber Harvest Area in Alaska limiting timber harvest to only 20 percent of the total national forest's 17 million acres, or 3 million acres, for the next century, allowing only 30,000 acres to be harvested per year. The Tongass Timber Harvest Area is to be the first unit of the National Timber Harvest System designed to promote proper economic forestry practices on the federal lands as outlined in Goal Number Ten.

6. Creation of a National Mining System by Congressional authorization, to embody all provisions of the General Mining Act of 1872 with the added provision that all public lands including wilderness and national parks shall be open to mineral and energy production under wise use technologies in the interest of domestic economies and in the interest of national security.

7. Passage of the Beneficial Use Water Rights

Act to embody all the provisions of the Water Act of 1866 with the added provisions that Congress shall recognize as sovereign the rights of states in all matters related to the regulation and distribution of all waters originating in or passing through the states, and that the federal government shall not retain "reserved" or other federal property rights in waters arising on federal lands for which it cannot demonstrate beneficial use.

8. **Commemorate the 100th Anniversary of the founding of the Forest Reserves by William Steele Holman** who introduced the Section 24 rider to the Forest Reserve Act of 1891. This commemoration shall emphasize the homestead act of 1888 from which the Section 24 rider was derived and the commodity use and homestead settlement intent behind the law that created the national forests.

9. **The Rural Community Stability Act** shall give statutory authority to enable the U.S. Forest Service to offer a reasonable fraction of the timber on each ranger district in timber sales for the sole and proper purpose of promoting rural timber-dependent community stability, exempt from administrative appeal.

The Forest Service shall offer an adequate amount of timber from each Ranger District in the United States National Forest System to meet market demands up to the biological capacity of the district and sell such timber only to local logging firms and milling firms.

The first timber sales allowed under the provisions of this act shall be those designed to recapture accrued undercuts from previous years when the annual allowable harvest level has not been achieved.

10. Creation of a National Timber Harvest System by Congressional authorization, to identify and preserve for commodity use those timberlands suitable for sustained yield timber growth. Repeals non-declining, even-flow strictures of the Forest and Range Renewable Resource Planning Act of 1974 as amended by the National Forest Management Act of 1976. Identifies wise use technologies acceptable to harvest timber in the interest of domestic economies and in the interest of national security. Applies the Multiple Use - Sustained Yield Act of 1960 provisions that lands will be managed in "not necessarily the combination of uses that will give the greatest dollar return of the greatest unit output," so that no timber harvest plan may be identified as "below cost." No enactment is to impair the agency's ability to manage the National Timber Harvest System for timber harvest.

The Tongass Timber Harvest Area should be the first dedicated single-use timber harvest area in America's National Timber Harvest System, to consist of the 3 million acres identified by the TLMP II planning process as suitable for growing commercial timber. Such areas should permit Multiple Use recreation where feasible. The Tongass timber industry should have all its former logging lands restored to logging status for the 100 year rotation so that at least 20 percent of the Tongass is scheduled for timber harvest over the next 100 years.

11. National Parks Reform Act, to create protective agencies for our natural heritage of a size conducive to responsible management and accessible to congressional oversight. Creates within the Department of the Interior, under authority of the Assistant Secretary for Fish and Wildlife and Parks four separate agencies each with its own director responsible for management of our current oversized and jumbled national park system: Reorganizes the National Park Service, with new management responsibility limited to only those units officially designated "national parks" and "national monuments" in the "natural" category; creates the National Urban Park Service with management responsibility for all units of the park system in urban settings designed primarily for contemplation, enlightenment or inspiration such as the National Capitol Parks; creates the National Recreational Park Service with management responsibility for all National Recreation Areas of the park system and other units primarily used for recreational purposes; creates the National Historical Park Service with management responsibility for all national historic parks and similar units of primarily historic interest.

The present National Park Service with its domain in excess of 80 million acres has grown into a bureaucracy so huge and powerful that it can ignore the public will, the intent of Congress and direct orders of the Secretary of the Interior with impunity. Such concentrated power cannot be allowed to persist within a representative form of government. This Act will separate out from the present conglomeration of diverse units four different kinds of national heritage lands that have previously been lumped together into a single vast and unresponsive agency. The new arrangement will group together those that are naturally similar for appropriate management to protect the essential character of each different kind of park.

MISSION 2010: Adequate Park Visitor Accommodations. A major thrust should be made to properly accommodate the increased visitor load on our parks through a 20-year construction program of new concessions including overnight accommodations, classic rustic lodges, campgrounds and visitor service stores in all 48 national parks, with priority given to Great Smoky Mountain, Everglades, Rocky Mountain, Big Bend, Canyonlands, Sequoia, Redwoods, North Cascades, Denali, and Theodore Roosevelt. Concession restoration should begin immediately in Yellowstone (West Thumb). The lodge at Manzanita Lake in Lassen Volcanic National Park, which was demolished by the National Park Service, shall be rebuilt in replica on its original site and become the first project of Mission 2010, to become known as the Don Hummel Memorial Lodge honoring the late outstanding leader of the national park concession movement. The Concession Policy Act of 1965 should be extended to all facilities of the proposed four park services.

Appropriate overnight visitor facilities should be constructed in all national monuments, national recreation areas, and major historical areas. Policies that exclude people shall be outlawed. The possessory interest of the private concessioner firms now serving the visiting public should be maximized. Private firms with expertise in people-moving such as Walt Disney should be selected as new transportation concessioners to accommodate and enhance the national park experience for all visitors without degrading the environment.

All actions designed to exclude park visitors such as shutting down overnight accommodations and rationing entry should be stopped as inimical to the mandate of Congress for "public use and enjoyment" in the National Park Act of 1916.

12. Pre-Patent Protection of Pest Control Chemicals. The patent clock on newly discovered pest control chemicals should start running only after government-imposed regulation-compliance requirements have been met. Since the testing period for new chemical approvals typically exceeds three years, during which the owner of the chemical can realize no income on investment, it is only fair that patents run from the time an innovation becomes marketable, yet pre-patent protection should be granted as a matter of governmental duty.

13. **Create the National Rangeland Grazing System.** Congress should authorize a National Rangeland Grazing System on all federal lands presently under permit according to the terms of the Taylor Grazing Act [43 U.S.C. 315-315(o)], or managed as rangeland under the Federal Land Policy and Management Act of 1976 [43 U.S.C. 1701-1782] or other applicable rangeland statute, and which (1) generally contains split estate values of privately owned possessory interests in the Federal lands, including but not limited to: water rights, range rights, privately owned range improvements such as roads, fences, stock watering facilities, ranch houses, cook houses, and bunk houses, (2) is rendered more valuable by the contribution of commensurable private land, (3) is biologically suited to grazing by either intensive or extensive livestock management methods, and (4) may also be available to multiple use for purposes including but not limited to hunting, hiking, motorized recreation, watershed management, wildlife management, timber harvest and minerals management but no application shall impair the operation of the rangeland as livestock grazing areas.

14. **Compassionate Wilderness Policy.** The Veterans and Handicapped Wilderness Provision should be enacted by statute to allow motorized wheel chairs into all Wilderness Areas in the National Wilderness Preservation System.

15. **National Industrial Policy Act.** Enact the following provision: "all agencies of the Federal Government shall include in every recommendation or report on proposals for legislation and other

major Federal actions significantly affecting the
quality of the human environment, a detailed statement by the responsible official:
    (vi) the economic impact of delaying or deny-
ing the proposed action,
    (vii) the economic benefits of immediately
going forward with the proposed action.

16. Truth In Regulation Act. In all agency plans
that presently combine the production costs with
overhead costs of a Federal action such as the
offering of a timber sale on a national forest, all non-
production costs shall be identified separately and
conspicuously, including costs of writing the NEPA
Environmental Impact Statement, costs of comply-
ing with environmental regulations on the ground,
costs of government buildings, vehicles and utilities
required to complete the plan, and salaries and
benefits of all agency staff employed in the project.

17. Property Rights Protection. Railroad easements when abandoned by the original or successor
railroad operating company, shall revert to the
underlying adjacent property owner. No easement
shall be given by government decree to a "Rails-to-
Trails" program without payment of just compensation plus money damages for loss of economic opportunity.

18. Endangered Species Act Amendments. The
Endangered Species Act shall be amended to specifically classify the appropriate scientifically identified endangered species as relict species in decline
before the appearance of man, including non-adap-
tive species such as the California Condor, and
endemic species lacking the biological vigor to spread
in range such as the wildflower Pipers harebells of
the Olympic mountains. Federal projects designed
to protect species identified as relicts shall require

a report stating all costs, separate and cumulative, of protecting the relict species, including computations of lost economic opportunities for projects denied because of the relict species.

All costs associated with mitigation and protection efforts required by federal law to protect endangered species shall be fully identified, separated from accounting statements and documented and made available for public inspection in an annual report to the Congress to be filed by the Secretaries of affected departments.

Hiding, disguising or willfully concealing the existence of an endangered species protection cost shall be a felony malfeasance of office subject to severe penalties of fine and imprisonment.

19. Obstructionism Liability. Any group or individual that challenges by litigation an economic action or development on federal lands and subsequently loses in court shall be declared "not acting in the public interest" and shall be required to pay to the winner the increase in costs for completing the project plus money damages for loss of economic opportunity.

Congress should provide for obstructionists to indemnify American industry against harm when they use the law to delay economic progress. The law must require that those who bring administrative appeals or court actions against timber harvest plans, mining plans, grazing plans, petroleum exploration or development plans or other commodity uses of federal lands shall post bonds equivalent to the economic benefits to be derived from the challenged harvest plus cost overruns caused by delay. If the appellant or plaintiff loses, payment in full is to be made to the defendant in proportion to his losses and expenses.

20. Private Rights In Federal Lands Act

Congress should enact measures which recognize that private parties legitimately own possessory rights to timber contracts, mining claims, water rights, grazing permits and other claims that are recognized by the several states and by Internal Revenue Service estate tax collection policy as valuable private property rights. Establishes the principle of the Private Domain in Federal Land.

21. Global Resources Wise Use Act

Congress should enact a policy measure that explicitly recognizes the shrinking relative size of the total goods sector of our world's economy and takes steps to insure raw material supplies for global commodity industries on a permanent basis. Should include free trade measures and incentives for developing nations that favor private enterprise. Should provide for technology exchange of wise use methods and a global data bank of technical information on sustainable resource development processes including prevention and cleanup techniques.

22. Perfect the Wilderness Act.

The National Wilderness Preservation System must be reassessed and reclassified into more carefully targeted categories according to the actual appropriate use, including:

1) Human Exclosures, areas where people are prohibited altogether, including wildlife scientists who frequently harass to death the very animals they are supposed to protect;

2) Wild Solitude Lands, managed exactly as present Wilderness areas;

3) Backcountry Areas, which allow widely spaced hostels, primitive toilets to prevent unsanitary conditions that prevail today along Wilderness trails, and higher trail standards to prevent the trail erosion that plagues current Wilderness areas;

4) Frontcountry, to allow primitive and developed campsites, motorized trail travel and limited commercial development;

5) Commodity Use Areas, which will allow all commodity industry uses on an as-needed basis in times of high demand. The present Wilderness System would be redesignated with approximately 1 million acres of scattered Human Exclosures; 20 million acres of Wild Solitude Lands; 30 million acres of Backcountry; 30 million acres of Frontcountry; and 10 million acres of Commodity Use Areas.

Congress must also address the serious question of continuing to operate the National Wilderness Preservation System at a deficit. Vast amounts of natural resources are contained within Wilderness boundaries and substantial annual appropriations go to maintain hiking trails, camp sites, fire rings, horse rails, primitive toilets and other facilities, and large amounts of taxpayer money go into studies of Wilderness, yet the Wilderness system has operated at a deficit every year since it was established in 1964. A Wilderness User fee must be established comparable to the entry fee program employed by the National Park Service. Wilderness is not a free good. It costs all taxpayers and benefits only a small minority. Only the affluent and well educated use Wilderness areas. Fewer than .01 percent of all Wilderness users consist of the educationally and economically disadvantaged. Wilderness users should pay for their recreation.

23. Standing To Sue In Defense Of Industry.
Just as environmentalists won standing to sue on behalf of scenic, recreational and historic values in the 1965 case *Scenic Hudson Preservation Conference v. Federal Power Commission*, so pro-industry advocates should win standing to sue on behalf of industries threatened or harmed by environmentalists. Today, a specific individual or firm that is

harmed must join a lawsuit as a plaintiff and pro-
industry advocacy groups such as the Center for the
Defense of Free Enterprise cannot bring a lawsuit
as a party of interest, despite their years of advocacy
in support of business and industry. Because industries must continue to live with their regulators
after lawsuits are settled they are hesitant to bring
legal action in all but the most horrendous circumstances, which chills their access to justice. Just as
Scenic Hudson conferred standing to sue on organizations devoted to saving natural features, recognizing them as harmed parties, so our court system
must confer standing to sue on organizations devoted to saving industry, recognizing them as harmed
parties. There is no symmetry today between the
rights of environmentalists to sue and the rights of
pro-industry advocates to sue. This is not fair and
must be changed in the name of justice.

24. National Recreation Trails Trust Fund.
Trail enthusiasts using motorized vehicles pay
millions in federal gasoline taxes annually which
are used to construct highways, not aid motorized
recreation programs. These monies should instead
be returned to a National Recreational Trails Trust
Found. The fund would provide matching grants to
state and federal land management agencies, and
local governments, coordinated through appropriate state agencies (state parks and recreation departments or departments of natural resources)
with the primary goal of encouraging multiple-use
trail development. A provision should also be made
for adding additional revenues to the fund in the
future, revenues derived from trail activities which
do not generate fuel taxes.

25. The End of the "Let Burn" Policy. All
naturally-caused wildfires in national park units
and wilderness areas will be immediately and effec-

tively extinguished to prevent the loss of natural and economic values. More importantly, all ground fuel accumulations which could lead to disastrous wildfires shall be actively prevented by a wise use management program.

Wildfire Prevention. All national park and wilderness areas will be managed to prevent the long-term buildup of ground fuels such as dead and down trees that create the ignition base for wildfires. Prevention must be actively pursued on all areas and is not optional. Prevention techniques may be of two kinds, to be permitted by temporary suspension of the Wilderness Act of 1964 in affected areas to allow motorized vehicles proper economic and rational access to danger sites:

1) Managed Fuel-Reduction Burning. Fuel accumulations of dead and down wood in all national parks and wilderness areas will be periodically inspected, gathered and moved by tractor into appropriate batches and burned in accordance with state forestry regulations. Areas will be restored to pre-burn condition within two calendar years after managed fuel-reduction burning by hand raking crews and planting the affected area in fast-growing native indigenous herbaceous ground cover plants.

2) Commercial Fuel-Reduction Harvest. Fuel accumulations of dead and down wood in all national parks and wilderness areas will be periodically inspected, gathered and chipped by motorized portable equipment, and the chipped wood removed from the natural area. Chip transport trucks shall take the chips to the nearest mill willing to buy the chips and sold at market prices. Areas will be restored to pre-chipping condition within two calendar years after commercial fuel-reduction harvest by hand raking crews and planting the affected area in fast-growing native indigenous herbaceous ground cover plants.

The neglect by any national park or wilderness administrator of ground fuel accumulations shall be a felony malfeasance of office subject to severe penalties of fine and imprisonment. A ground fuel wildfire, but not a crown fire, on any national park or wilderness area shall be prima facie evidence of negligence and malfeasance.

With such practical and beneficial techniques ready to hand there is no excuse for such disasters as the Yellowstone Holocaust of 1988.

SECTION II
LETTERS TO
PRESIDENT BUSH

**National Council for
Environmental Balance**
Louisville, Kentucky

Dear President Bush,

We appreciate this opportunity to report to you the findings of our organization on environmental matters. The following is our statement for inclusion in the Wise Use Agenda:

I. SCOPE OF GLOBAL ENVIRONMENTAL INTERESTS

National and world concern over environmental issues has riveted the attention of a very sizeable segment of the American population. There is little or no public opposition to any policy offered as protection for the environment, but unfortunately, there is considerable controversy over what constitutes a significant degree of environmental degradation, what control measures are needed, and what such control might actually achieve.

Sadly, a large measure of what has taken place in the name of environmental protection was grounded in little substantive knowledge compared to the hype that it received from various self-serving interests that thrive on uncertainty and alarmism. For example, today's early and incomplete indications of potentially serious problems with the greenhouse effect, the stability of the upper ozone layer, and acid rain are insufficiently understood to make informed decisions. The first two well-illustrate the inadequacy of public information, since both have aroused substantial alarm yet neither of them constitutes any immediate threat to present human affairs, although in the third instance certain acidified lakes have indeed lost their fish populations. The importance of the first two lies in the fact that in theory they pose the possibility of intense, worldwide and devastating change that could impair human and all other life, animal and plant, as it is now known.

The response to indications of this kind must be a substantive scientific effort to be sure that the U.S. (and the world) is aware of what is and is not taking place and is alert to appropriate corrective measures to be undertaken, if and when circumstances warrant. Other comparable global problems or potential problems exist (especially in the seas) with respect to which sufficient monitoring and exploration is essential lest the world be suddenly surprised by some unanticipated catastrophic trend. Our national effort must be adequate for our own purposes as well as our participation in such international cooperative efforts as might be undertaken.

II. NATIONAL AND LOCAL POLLUTION ISSUES

Compared to global problems, those within

regional, national or local boundaries are somewhat less complex and are better understood in terms of their sources, distribution and impacts. The public is more alert to national and local pollution issues since they perceive a personal association with some phase of a problem especially one bearing on their personal health and welfare. Even where no personal sense of hazard is present, the public has very properly been alerted to "what if...." Unfortunately, in this area, what information has reached the public has been almost totally slanted toward fear of a remote possibility of risk, magnified in most cases out of all proportion to reality, generally reported with all the outward appearances of a crisis.

Issues falling within this category abound and have been the driving force behind most of our environmental legislation. As a result, governments have passed numerous very costly yet unproductive environmental programs. In the area of pollution, failure to develop a sufficient knowledge of a candidate pollutant and an intimate understanding of the variety of human health implications has led to setting unreasonably restrictive ambient tolerance levels of certain substances or even outright bans on others for inadequate reasons, while truly dangerous practices with truly dangerous substances remain unmanaged.

The lack of public comprehension of the irrationality of regulatory efforts has been revealed during the past several years. Most significantly, Dr. N. Bruce Ames convinced Barbara Walters and Hugh Downs on ABC News' March 18, 1988 *20/20* broadcast that they had failed to report many significant facts about allegedly cancer producing chemicals, for example, that a large array of known cancer-causing agents occur naturally in ordinary fruits and vegetables, and have no connection to pesticide application or any other "tampering" by

man. Trace amounts of a chemical in prepared
products are banned while the same or larger doses
of an equivalent chemical in naturally occurring
foods are ignored, reflecting the irrationality of
regulatory efforts. Earlier, Edith Efron's book *The
Apocalyptics* presented voluminous evidence on the
same subject but to less avail than Dr. Ames' brief
appearance on TV.

This *20/20* illustration depicts only one of
many "pollution" issues about which the public is
inadequately informed to make intelligent decisions. Quite clearly, just as in the cases of the
greenhouse effect and ozone depletion alarms, we
need a firm scientific base upon which to inform the
public. Current cries of "greenhouse" are based
upon weather records so incomplete that many
reputable scientists can neither detect a real trend
toward global warming nor attribute it with any
certainty to carbon dioxide buildup in the atmosphere. Experiments indicating a connection of the
periodic ozone "hole" over Antarctica with fluorocarbons have included no control studies to explain
why the ozone does not thin or disappear in other
geographic areas where fluorocarbons are present
in the same quantities. The alarm over today's
incomplete knowledge of these issues is politically
motivated. So many false alarms of global disaster
have been published that the public is growing
cynical about any alarm, a very dangerous social
situation. In order to assure scientific integrity,
those charged with searching for the facts needs to
be isolated from dictation by any regulatory bureaucracy and free from the influence of those with
ideological devotion to public organizations that
capitalize on catastrophe theories.

With the facts in hand, our scientists and
technologists will have what is needed to propose
sensible environmental solutions and to submit
reasonable alternatives for public decision.

III. ENVIRONMENTAL PRIORITIES

It is essential that public confidence be restored in our ability to deal effectively with environmental problems. To that end we must develop a system of priorities that will assure us that whatever resources are applied to environmental protection are allocated to genuine problems and not squandered on will-o'-the-wisp programs derived from some "disaster of the month" club. The solution is to undertake basic fact-finding independent of special interests, whether they be political, commercial or bureaucratic. The cliché that we can undertake unlimited pollution control and prevent any and all environmental degradation on any and all fronts must be tempered with a degree of realism, a need which so far has escaped public attention. In the turmoil of our legislative panic, we seem to have lost sight of the basic fact that pollution of any kind is a matter of form and logistics and that technology does not create any matter that was not present to begin with. With that absolute scientific fact in mind, "waste" returned to its original site is essentially the restoration of "nature." Only as technology relocates and concentrates nature's materials and misplaces them do they constitute an increased hazard.

Ideally, therefore, our number one priority must be for resource conservation, recycling and restoration. Conservation in this context does not mean preservation or non-use. With this basic principle in mind, it is clear that the key to pollution control is the availability of an abundant and economical supply of energy, raw materials and suitable technology. Thus the concentration, conversion, transport and storage of pollutants, whether from air, water or soil, are seen to be highly energy dependent, which can be considered the common denominator of any control measures. Appropriate technology that minimizes the energy cost of pollu-

tion control needs to be a primary goal for a successful program that protects both ecology and economy.

IV. THE IMPACT OF POLLUTANTS ON HEALTH AND HUMAN WELFARE

Man's primary personal concern with pollution is its impact on human health. The present
U.S. health policy is to extend absolute protection to
the most susceptible individual (zero risk), a target
which upon thoughtful analysis by medical specialists is recognized as unattainable for the simple
reason that nature in its purest form routinely pres-
ents extreme risks to even the hardiest individual.
Our humanitarian instincts thus lead us to stop all
the processes of civilization that sustain us in order
to prevent the unpreventable.

Political scientist Aaron Wildavsky has perti-
nently commented:

> How extraordinary! The rich-
> est, longest-lived, best-protected, most
> resourceful civilization, with the high-
> est degree of insight into its own tech-
> nology, is on the way to becoming the
> most frightened. Has there ever been,
> one wonders, a society that produced
> more uncertainty more often about
> everyday life? [Uncertainty about]...the
> land we live on, the water we drink,
> the air we breathe, the food we eat, the
> energy that supports us. Chicken Little
> is alive and well in America.

An enlightened and more circumspect plan
for guarding our health from environmental effects
must be developed. The direction of that development must be in competent hands and free of political or bureaucratic domination.

V. PUBLIC AWARENESS

The American public is not aware of the huge economic and social costs of environmental projects. The hundreds of billions of dollars that go into pollution control programs and the lost-opportunity costs of stopping the use of natural resources on public lands is nowhere separated from the overall bookkeeping of any corporation or government. The huge increase of invisible costs for goods and services throughout the economy attributable to environmental programs cannot be identified. We simply do not know what it costs to enforce the hundreds of environmental laws now on the books. The public blithely accepts the popular but fallacious view that environmental problems are easily handled and that the costs are trifling compared to the infinite benefits gained. The public, furthermore, naively considers the costs to be paid only from corporate profits or government with none accruing to the public.

It is time to require accountability for each and every environmental program administered by every level of government. This accountability must explicitly state the costs and actual results of the program, so that the public can decide whether to retain the law or repeal it.

VI. EDUCATIONAL NEEDS

Public opinion on the environment today is based upon scant, absent and even fraudulent information. A full-scale program to correct this deficiency is essential. Much scientific data on environmental problems is readily available but not provided to the public for these reasons:

1. The inclination of the media to selectively report only bad news and ignore good news.

2. The political orientation of the media to favor government intervention rather than market-oriented or other alternative non-coercive environ-

mental improvement programs.

3. Failure of scientists to fully express themselves publicly in order not to jeopardize grant
prospects by stating facts that might be inconven-
ient for the ideological program of foundations or
environmental organizations.

4. Organizations that capitalize on environmental disaster threats for political and fund raising purposes have deliberately distorted information and create false public perceptions of environmental issues.

The rectification of this deplorable situation
will require careful planning and a comprehensive
program with vigorous sponsorship.

Irwin Tucker, Ph.D.
Executive Director

Southeastern Utah Association of Local
Governments
Price, Utah

Dear President Bush,
The Wise Use Agenda contributions by Southeastern Utah Association of Local Governments are
as follows:

TRANSPORTATION
1. Rights of counties to maintain, improve or
otherwise modify roads constructed under authority of Revised Statute 2477 shall not be and are not
abridged, diminished or abrogated by any subsequent act of congress including but not limited to the
Wilderness Act, the Federal Land Policy Management Act, and the National Environmental Policy
Act.

2. It shall be the policy of congress to support
and encourage the construction of all weather loop

roads, scenic highways and associated amenities on the public lands to accommodate the increasing number of older recreationists and working families with limited time available who seek experience on the public lands by motorized or mechanized means.

ENERGY

All public lands shall be left open to mineral and energy production in the interest of domestic economies and in the interest of national security.

WILDERNESS IMPACT

1. All states with federal ownership of the land base in excess of twenty-five percent shall be exempt from provisions of the Wilderness Act of 1964.

2. Congress shall recognize as sovereign the rights of states in all matters related to the regulation and distribution of all waters originating in or passing through the states.

3. In the interest of viable domestic economies and national security, as well as to protect valid existing rights and historic uses, congress repudiates any concept of protective perimeters or buffer zones surrounding federally withdrawn areas to include but not be limited to national parks and wilderness areas.

4. The designation of wilderness areas in national parks is supported with the provision that environmentally sensitive, all weather roads be constructed through such areas to allow access to the general public, consistent with the purpose of the parks and to minimize the impact by concentrating it in localized areas.

OBSTRUCTIONISM

Judicial or administrative appellants of proposed projects on federal lands shall be required to post bonds equal to the cost of the proposed project plus added costs for delays and legal fees with payments to be made to the defendant when the defendant prevails and in proportion to his losses and expenses.

COMMUNITY STABILITY

Congress recognized that rural communities surrounded by federal lands are in large measure dependent upon those lands for their economic stability. Congress, therefore, reaffirms and directs all federal land managers to recognize that comments on federal land management planning initiatives are to be given priority consideration in the public comment process.

MINERALS POLICY

1. Congress recognizes the need for a national energy policy which maintains federal lands as available for mineral and energy exploration and development in the interest of viable domestic economies and national security.

2. Congress recognizes the wisdom and utility of the 1872 mining law and hereby asserts its intent to maintain this law without change, including current fees for filing annual assessment notices.

3. Congress rejects the notion of a five dollar filing fee per claim per year as being excessive, punitive and contrary to the best interests of local economies and national security.

4. Congress supports the concept of maintaining public lands under multiple use and sustained yield principles in order to foster energy and mineral production in response to market conditions and other changes. Accordingly, congress recognizes the necessity of holding to a minimum the amount of land relegated to a single purpose such as wilderness and national parks.

GRAZING POLICY

Grazing shall remain an accepted use on public land with rates or fees commensurate with values after considering all related market conditions.

TOXIC MATERIALS POLICY

States shall have primacy in the management of toxic substances within their borders provided that strict adherence be maintained to all applicable federal laws.

PRIVATIZATION

All services provided on federal lands including parks and monuments shall be provided by the private sector in-so-far as practicable.

CRITICAL ECO/ECONOSYSTEMS

Congress recognizes that land dependent domestic economies are a legitimate component of a viable ecosystem. Accordingly, congress recognizes the necessity for giving commentary from local communities priority consideration in the public comment phase of federal land management planning.

WILD AND SCENIC RIVERS

Congress subordinates its authority for the designation of wild and scenic rivers to the states.

OTHER RECOMMENDATIONS

1. Congress recognizes the seasonal burdens placed on local economies as a consequence of recreation on federal lands. Accordingly, congress recognizes the necessity for calculating federal payments-in-lieu-of-taxes on both the indigenous population and upon the estimated itinerant population attached to an area in pursuit of recreation on federal lands.

2. Congress recognizes that improved or newly constructed facilities, particularly roads, relieve human impacts on federal lands by concentrating use in areas adapted to that purpose and by giving people the opportunity to view and experience the land without deeply penetrating the land and thereby heavily impacting it. Accordingly, congress supports the notion of sensitively constructed all weather roads in federal wilderness areas and units of the national park service. This approach makes these lands available to the general public, as they should be, while maintaining the pristine character of the land and its floral and faunal communities.

3. Primitive and semi primitive recreationists have been successful in having large areas of public domain set aside for their use to the exclusion of other uses. These lands require management and, therefore, incur a cost borne by the general public. Congress recognizes this inequitable circumstance. Accordingly, congress supports the notion of a Human Use Fee or Human Use Permit to be charged to or purchased by those who seek to recreate on such lands as wilderness, national parks, primitive areas, and ROSP and SPNM class areas.

4. Congress recognizes that an unresolved conflict exists between current federal land management policies which restrict economic and/ or commodity production and the bilateral compact between the federal government and the states which require that revenues from state trust lands be maximized for the benefit of designated beneficiaries. The existence of state trust lands, as well as other communities of interest, requires that congress reconsider the Wilderness Act, the National Environmental Policy Act and the Federal Land Policy Management Act.

William D. Howell, Executive Director, Southeastern Utah Association of Local Governments.

Hannibal Hamlin Institute for Economic Policy Studies
Hallowell, Maine

Dear President Bush,

It is my pleasure on behalf fo the Hannibal Hamlin Institute for Economic Policy Studies to participate in this project. Enclosed you will find our recommendation for inclusion in The Wise Use Agenda.

FEDERALISM AND ENVIRONMENT

Recommendation:

The Bush Administration should adopt a policy of environmental federalism which recognizes the appropriate federal and state government responsibilities governing products in interstate commerce.

Products sold in interstate commerce should, where necessary, be subject only to federal requirements and not to a mosaic of diverse and conflicting state laws which unnecessarily impede commerce, escalate costs, diminish the effectiveness and reliability of consumer information and erode American economic competitiveness.

State toxics initiatives such as California's Proposition 65 (The Safe Drinking Water and Toxics Enforcement Act of 1986) should be viewed as violating the principles of environmental federalism.

Background:

For the last 20 years, the United States has been in the throes of an environmental revolution that has raised awareness and concern for the utilization of natural recourses and the impact 'of potentially toxic substances on the air, water, land, wildlife and human environments.

This environmental revolution has resulted in far-reaching federal legislation such as the Clean Air Act, the Clean Water Act, the Superfund Act, the Toxics Substances Control Act and numerous other statutory requirements for safe and effective use of America's resources. While the efficacy of these Acts may be debated, they have nonetheless created a comprehensive federal framework within which consumers, manufacturers, retailers and government may operate.

Recently, state governments have moved to overlay federal requirements with respect to environmental policy. When these laws address problems of state origin and responsibility, such as the clean-up of waste disposal sites, they reflect the constitutional role and right of state government. However, when these state laws address products in interstate commerce, they violate federalism and impose arbitrary, unnecessary economic and societal costs that should not be tolerated.

Matthew J. Glavin
President.

California Women In Timber

Dear President Bush,

Trees are one of America's renewable natural resources. Our national forests should be managed for multiple-use, balancing recreation and timber production. It is important that we maximize timber growth and increase timberland productivity in order to supply the people of our nation with the wood products they need.

The following criteria should be considered in the management of our national forests:

● Our national forests must be managed for

sustained yield timber production.

● Timber harvest levels should be based on what the land base can biologically produce given mandated forest constraints.

● Forest plans must be developed and implemented in a timely manner in accordance with the law.

● Timber output should at least equal Forest and Rangeland Renewable Resource Planning Act of 1974 (RPA) goals set for each region.

● Community stability and the economic well-being of local communities must be considered when developing forest plans.

● The Forest Service should use their expertise to educate the general public on the differences in meaning between national forests, national parks, and wilderness. The meanings of these terms cause much confusion in the minds of the average American citizen. People must be educated about the restrictions associated with wilderness designation; and the benefits and rewards that can be derived from wise multiple-use of our national forests.

Acreage contained in our national parks and in wilderness areas is more than adequate. Existing parklands should be developed and maintained with no more new acreage set aside.

The Membership - California Women In Timber

American Freedom Coalition
Washington, D.C.

Dear President Bush,
After speaking with Merrill Sikorski, the Director of our Environmental Task Force, he asked that I send you this statement for the Agenda for the

Wise Use of the Environment:

        The American Freedom Coalition's Task Force
on the Environment is committed to protecting
Earth's environment and wise use of our natural
resources to promote economic growth and human
progress while assuring protection from pollution,
overuse, and depletion. We therefore support legislation that would authorize the Secretary of the
Interior to lease, in an expeditious and environmentally sound manner, the 1.5 million acre Coastal
Plain of Alaska's National Wildlife Refuge (ANWR)
for oil and gas exploration.
        In order to lessen our reliance on imported
oil, America must rely on both greater conservation
and the development of oil and gas resources that
might be found on the ANWR Coastal Plain.
        The national defense and energy security of
the United States will be greatly enhanced if major
petroleum reserves are discovered and developed.

Michael F. Beard
National Field Director

T.E.A.M. Taxpayers for the Environment
And its Management
Scotia, California

Dear President Bush,
        The decision-making process on our public
lands, including national forests, needs to be revised.
        All policy development should be based upon
factually reliable studies. Only scientific reports
that have been properly replicated to assure reliability should form the basis for each federal policy.
No study which has originated from a special inter-

est lobby should be allowed to stand by itself, but should be considered only if opposing interests have had an opportunity to submit comparable data.

Priority must be given to local legislation and management of natural resources to ensure economic stability and credibility. Federal policy must follow local policy, not lead it.

Only local judicial units should be permitted to review appeals on resource management disputes. Judges' schools should be instituted on community stability issues.

Government agencies should be required to provide a minimum of one year for regional study and local public input before allocating or approving any tax funds for wilderness designation or private land acquisition.

Gary Gundlach
Janet C. Baird
T.E.A.M. Organizers

National Rifle Association of America
Washington, D.C.

Dear President Bush,

WHEREAS, Lawful hunting has been significantly curtailed by certain unreasonable regulations adopted as a result of the expansion of the National Wilderness System and National Park System; and

WHEREAS, These arbitrary and capricious regulations in fact do not promote the interests of wildlife conservation or the responsible public enjoyment of wilderness lands, contrary to the intent of Congress; and

WHEREAS, The National Rifle Association of America in fulfillment of its purposes to promote hunting and the conservation and wise use of our renewable wildlife resources has become increasingly concerned with this abridgement of the rights of law-abiding citizens; now, therefore, be it

RESOLVED, That the National Rifle Association of America opposes any further expansion of the National Wilderness System and National Park System and implementing regulations that do not adequately recognize and preserve existing hunting access and opportunities; and, be it further

RESOLVED, That the National Rifle Association of America supports the restoration of hunting access and sound wildlife management practices in such areas where they have been improperly curtailed.

Passed by the Board of Directors of the National Rifle Association of America in meeting assembled the 27th day of April, 1987 in Reno, Nevada

Blue Ribbon Coalition Inc.
Pocatello, Idaho

Dear President Bush,

National Recreation Trails Trust Fund

Americans today spend more time and more dollars on recreation than ever before. At the same time, the number of different recreational activities has soared. This increase in recreation is very evident on America's trails but in many cases this expanded demand has not been matched by expanded supply. The result has been a growing problem in providing quality trail experiences.

Snowmobiles, trailbikes (motorcycles) dual purpose motorcycles, and ATV's represent one of the fastest growing recreational interests in America. There has been a very positive impact on our national economy as a result of the growth of the distribution facilities, dealer networks, repair shops, and in some cases manufacturers of these off highway vehicles (OHV's).

Some states have recognized the value of establishing state registration programs to help provide facilities for the growing OHV user population. Incorporated into the most successful state programs has been the provision for that portion of the state gasoline tax that is estimated to be used off highway to be deposited into these programs. The President's Commission on Americans Outdoors recognized the effectiveness of these programs and recommended that federal fuel tax receipts generated by motorized vehicles used off-highway be used to aid recreation.

Trail enthusiasts using motorized vehicles pay millions in federal gasoline taxes annually which are used to construct highways, not aid motorized recreation programs. These monies should instead be returned to a National Recreational Trails Trust Found. The fund would provide matching grants to state and federal land management agencies, and local governments, coordinated through appropriate state agencies (state parks and rec. or DNR), with the primary goal of encouraging multiple-use trail development. A provision should also be made for additional revenues to the fund in the future, revenues derived from trail activities which do not generate fuel taxes.

Legislation establishing the National Recreation Trails Trust Fund should incorporate the following points:
● The U. S. Dept. of the Interior should administer the program using no more than 5% of annual receipts for dispersing funds and providing technical assistance. (We feel that 5% should be sufficient because the engineering, project inspection, and supervision should be handled at the state

rather than federal level.)

● The Dept. of the Treasury should determine the amount of federal taxes paid on fuel used in motorized recreation vehicles used off highway within five years after enactment, and periodically thereafter.

● Grants should be made available for trail development, maintenance, easement acquisition, and facility development.

● State eligibility for grants would be automatic for four years, and thereafter dependent upon:

I. State action to establish an OHV registration program that includes a set aside of state fuel taxes paid by motorized off-highway recreationists; and

II. Establishment of a state trail advisory board.

● Partnerships with private landowners would be encouraged.

● A national trails advisory board, representing trail users, and including federal officials as ex officio members, would be established.

● A maximum of 5% of the monies would be available for environmental and safety information programs.

● 50% of the available grant monies would be divided equally among eligible states.

● 50% of the available grant monies would be divided among eligible states based on the number of vehicles used off highway in each state.

● Monies not expended by a state within two years would be reclaimed, and would be available for redistribution to other states who are actively participating in the program.

WILDERNESS EFFECT ON RECREATION

Wilderness designation is not good for recreation. Wilderness proponents have been telling the American public they should support Wilderness because of the recreation opportunities they say it will provide. When asked to prove the benefits to recreation, they say it isn't for recreation, that these lands must be locked up. They must be saved for our children, and our children's children. In actuality, they want to lock up our public lands so our grandchildren can't use them either.

They complain about the timber industry, and then seek to have an area where they hike on old timber roads designated as Wilderness. They hate the mining industry, and seek Wilderness designation for an area where the chief attraction is an old abandoned mine. They have convinced many people that if our land managers are allowed to continue managing our public lands as they have in the past, they will be lost forever.

The Wilderness advocates have, for too long, portrayed themselves as representing recreation, when in fact they represent only a small percentage of the recreation public. They say primitive recreation should have priority, and must have exclusive use of large tracts of public land. They require solitude, and seek Congressional designation to guarantee it. They don't even want to see one another in the backcountry, let alone a cow or a trailbike. Multiple use to them is more than one hiker on a trail.

POLITICS

There are at least two ways to protect our public lands. The only method being promoted by the traditional environmentalist is to lock everyone else out. Let nature take its course, is what they propose. They prefer to see our forests fall in a tangle of deadfall, or burn, than to see them harvested. They say that only those with the time and physical capability to hike long distances deserve to see our back country. If you can't rough it, you don't deserve to enjoy these public lands.

We believe our public lands should be open to varied types of recreational activities, for all types of users, not just the few served by Wilderness designation. We believe that dispersed use and multiple use management offer resource protection and accommodate a growing recreational user public. Wilderness area promoters are not supporters of recreational activities. Wilderness classification contributes absolutely nothing to increase the recreational potential of an area.

Primitive recreationists say they support increased funding for recreational trails, but adamantly oppose trail improvements proposed to be paid for by dedicated ORV funds. They are afraid that might prohibit the area from being designated Wilderness. They promote a double standard. They call a two-foot-deep gully in the Wilderness a trail and a two-inch-deep rut in a multiple use trail unacceptable ORV damage.

Wilderness advocates are more concerned with increasing their political power than with protecting our environment. The public land use issue has become a contest, to see just how far they can go, and has little to do with protecting our natural resources.

Clark L. Collins
President and Executive Director.

FOR INCLUSION IN THE WISE USE AGENDA:

The following members of the Blue Ribbon Coalition support the wise use of our natural resources and subscribe to the philosophy of "preserving our natural resources FOR the public instead of

FROM the public."

SUBSCRIBED:

Alaska
Alaska Motorcycle Racing Association, Anchorage

Arizona
Arizona Desert Racing Association, Phoenix
Arizona Motorcycle Dealers Association,
Scottsdale
Arizona Outdoor Coalition, Tucson
Greenlee Public Lands Committee, Clifton

California
California-Nevada Snowmobile Association,
Placerville
Dirt Alert, Santa Clara
Motorcycle Industry Council
Western Chapter, International Snowmobile
Council, Rancho Cordova

Colorado
Colorado Motorcycle Dealers Association, Denver
Colorado Off Highway Vehicle Coalition, Littleton
Timberline Trailriders, Steamboat Springs

Idaho
Associated Logging Contractors of Idaho, Coeur
d'Alene
The Brush Bunch Motorcycle Club, Post Falls
Central Idaho Rod and Gun Club, Challis
Cougar Mountain Snowmobile Association, Boise
Idaho Cattle Association, Boise
Idaho Falls Trail Machine Association, Idaho
Falls
Idaho Forest Industries, Inc., Coeur d'Alene
Idaho Gem and Mineral Society, Twin Falls
Idaho Hunters Association, Boise

Idaho Public Land Users Association, Pocatello
Idaho Trail Machine Association, Boise
Idaho Snow Riders, Mountain Home
Idaho State Snowmobile Association, Boise
Idaho Wool Growers Association, Boise
Magic Valley Trail Machine Association,
Twin Falls
Magic Valley Snowmobilers, Inc., Twin Falls
North Idaho Trail Riders Organization, Wallace
Northwest Power Boat Association, Lewiston
Treasure Valley Trail Machine Association, Boise
Panhandle Snowmobile Association,
Bonners Ferry
Pocatello Trail Machine Association, Pocatello

Maine
Maine ATV Association, Augusta

Montana
Missoula Snowgoers, Missoula
Montana 4X4 Association, Bozeman
Montana Snowmobile Association, Helena
Montana Trail Bike Riders Association, Bozeman

Nevada
Wilderness Impact Research Foundation, Elko

New Mexico
Jackelopes Motorcycle Club, Taos
New Mexico Snowmobile Association,
Albuquerque
Santa Fe Trail Snowmobile Club, Santa Fe

Ohio
American Motorcyclist Association, Westerville

Oregon
Klamath Basin Snowdrifters, Klamath Falls
Motorcycle Riders Association, Medford

Oregon ATV Association, Coos Bay
Oregon State Snowmobile Association, Salem
Moon Country Snowmobilers, Inc., Bend
Northwest Road and Trail Association, Tigard

Utah
Utah ATV Association, West Valley City
Utah Snowmobile Association, Sandy
Utah Trail Machine Association, American Fork

Washington
Bremerton Cruisers, Bremerton
Eastern Washington Dirt Riders, Kennewick
Lake Chelan Snowmobile Association, Chelan
Northwest ATV Association, Monroe
Pacific Northwest Four Wheel Drive Association,
Longview
Ridgerunners ORV Club, Republic
Roadrunners Motorcycle Club, Tacoma
Skagit Motorcycle Club, Mount Vernon
Tacoma Motorcycle Club, Puyallup
Washington ATV Association, Enumclaw
Washington State Snowmobile Association,
Kirkland
Yakima Valley Dust Dodgers, Yakima

Wyoming
Casper Dirt Riders, Casper
Lander Snowdrifters, Lander
Sour Doughs Snowmobile Club, Lander
Sweetwater County Snowpokes, Rock Springs
Wyoming State Snowmobile Association, Pinedale
Wyoming Trail Machine Association, Story

[Editor's Note: The inclusion of these seventy groups from the Blue Ribbon Coalition's nationwide network reflects the Wise Use Movement's profound commitment to its active recreation constituency.]

Multiple Use Association
Gorham, New Hampshire

Dear President Bush,

   The Multiple Use Association is a grassroots membership group concerned about the needs of all forest users, the health of the forest now and in the future and the promotion of good forest management practices. The Forest Service has determined that less than five percent of the people who use national forests use Wilderness areas. One half of those Wilderness users would get as good or better experience in a multiple use area according to the USFS.
   Contrary to environmentalists' contentions that old growth forests possess values that second growth forests do not, a properly managed forest is healthier and more attractive. Younger trees are less susceptible to disease and insects. The forests of New Hampshire and Maine are attractive and healthy because they were harvested properly. To foster understanding in the general public we have distributed bumper stickers which read: Promote healthy forests - Support multiple use.

Leon Favreau
President

Trinity Resource Action Council
Weaverville, California

Dear President Bush,
   We are pleased to present this recommendation to the Wise Use Agenda.
GLOBAL WARMING AND THE GREENHOUSE EFFECT
   Global warming is caused by an increase in

atmospheric carbon dioxide resulting from the burning of fossil fuels and the deforestation of the earth. The carbon dioxide traps solar heat in the Earth's atmosphere causing temperatures to rise. We've had the five hottest years of the last century in the 1980s, and global temperatures are now the highest since mankind has been keeping records. The rate of global warming in the past two decades is higher than at any earlier recorded time. Has the greenhouse effect finally begun to take hold some 100 years after it was first predicted?

About half of the greenhouse effect is thought to be caused by a steady increase in atmospheric carbon dioxide. The main cause, an estimated 80%, is the conversion of fossilized forest remains (oil & coal) into energy, with the immediate release of carbon dioxide into the atmosphere. Another is the clearing and burning of tropical forest for agriculture, about 20%. There is another forest-related cause and that is the deforestation of the globe: an estimated 1.7 billion acres. So we have two forest factors: Deforestation of tropical rain forest to produce agricultural land and deforestation of rural forest to create large metropolitan areas.

This leads to the conclusion that people are deforesting the globe and causing the greenhouse effect. Yes, we are to blame. But before you push the panic button, man and mother nature are now working together to try to combat the problem of global warming.

First man: a national campaign introduced by the American Forestry Association in October, called "Global Releaf," is designed to encourage and assist Americans in planting 100 million trees in their communities by 1992. Global Releaf will show people that they can plant a tree and help cool the globe. There are an estimated 100 million energy efficient tree planting sites available around U.S. houses, towns and cities. How many of these energy efficient tree planting sites are in your community in unknown. But, stop for a minute and look outside of your home and/or business. Do you have well placed trees planted around your home or business? Three well placed trees per house can cut home air conditioning by 10 to 50 percent. Trees can create urban oases that are cool and more pleasant. As a result, planting urban trees can both reduce energy use and increase vegetation growth, a two way attack on the main causes of the greenhouse effect.

Mother nature's part in the solving or controlling of the greenhouse effect is through the natural process built into trees called photosynthesis. Trees, through their natural biological processes, take carbon dioxide out of the atmosphere, convert it to wood, and store it.

Global Releaf will involve everyone in every community including Trinity County and surrounding counties in California in its tree planting program. It will also call for other efforts, such as planting and managing rural forests, helping developing countries meet their social and economic challenges without destroying their forest and improving our understanding of global warming and its impacts through increased research.

So go out and plant a tree today. Show that you do care and are concerned about global warming. Replace a tree that is dead or dying, so that your own dwelling becomes more pleasant, your own energy use goes down, and you can say that you have done your part in solving global warming.

HEALTHY FORESTS MANUFACTURE OXYGEN

Forests act as a giant oxygen factory. Yes, a healthy forest not only contributes to the wood supply but also to the world's oxygen recycling system. Scientists calculate that for every ton of wood a forest grows, it removes 1.47 tons of carbon dioxide from the atmosphere and replaces it with

1.07 tons of oxygen a day.

So this wonderful device that converts carbon dioxide back into oxygen is no invention by any human mind. A healthy forest and a process called photosynthesis is the means by which our valuable air is replenished. Trees absorb water and minerals through their roots, transport them to the leaves or needles and come into contact with chlorophyll and air. Sunlight, passing through the leaves, comes in contact with the chlorophyll, breaking the water molecules apart. Oxygen from the broken water molecules is then exhausted through the leaf and into the air. Hydrogen from the water molecules combines with the carbon dioxide and produces a sugar which the trees use for food.

TRAC FACT: An average size healthy tree releases enough oxygen to supply the day-to-day needs of a family of four.

As a tree grows older, the requirement for sugar to grow decreases. Its photosynthetic production decreases and the tree releases less and less oxygen as time goes by. Eventually decay reverses the process so that oxygen is used in oxidizing decaying compounds from rot and disease and carbon dioxide is released into the atmosphere. Thus, an old growth tree becomes an oxygen user and carbon dioxide producer and thus part of the problem of global warming. So, by converting old growth forests to new forests we assure that young healthy trees will produce oxygen to battle the menace of carbon dioxide buildup.

If the American public and forest managers took advantage of the economically feasible opportunities to increase timber growth rates, the resulting increase in biological uptake of carbon dioxide could be equal to one-third of what we now release from burning fossil fuels. So, young healthy fast growing forests can contribute greatly to the oxygen supply while old growth forests use up oxygen and release carbon dioxide.

Richard Mabie, Jr.
Executive Director

Garfield County
Panguitch, Utah

Dear President Bush,
Please accept the following Garfield County policy statement for inclusion in THE WISE USE AGENDA. We sincerely hope that THE WISE USE AGENDA will have a positive impact on the new administration.

ACCESS TO PUBLIC LANDS
Garfield County, Utah recommends clear policy guidance to federal agencies which will clarify and define the rights of local governments to claim public rights of way under the provisions of Revised Statute 2477 (formerly codified at 43 CFR 932). This statute allows local governments to use, maintain and improve public roads which cross federal lands and existed prior to October 21, 1976.

WILDERNESS POLICY
Garfield County, Utah recommends that all future wilderness designations exclude areas containing resources necessary to the economic well-being of the affected local residents. Also, the management of designated wilderness areas must provide for the necessary public access to maintain resources including but not limited to water, minerals, timber, rangeland and intensive recreation uses.

SUSTAINED YIELD MULTIPLE USE PRINCIPLES
Garfield County, Utah is highly dependent

upon federal lands, which comprise 92.3 percent of the county land base. It is essential that these federal lands be managed so as to allow appropriate multiple uses. Attempts by narrow interest groups and federal agencies to restrict land uses on federal lands should be reviewed and closely coordinated with affected local governments.

We hope that these policy statements are a valuable addition to THE WISE USE AGENDA and wish you well in your efforts.

Thomas V. Hatch, Chairman
Garfield County Commission

Beaver County
Beaver, Utah

Dear President Bush,

Please accept the following Beaver County policy statement for including in THE WISE USE AGENDA. We sincerely hope that THE WISE USE AGENDA will have a positive impact on the new administration.

ACCESS TO PUBLIC LANDS

Beaver County, Utah recommends clear policy guidance to federal agencies which will clarify and define the rights of local governments to claim public rights of way under the provisions of Revised Statute 2477 (formerly codified at 43 CFR 932). This statute allows local governments to use, maintain and improve public roads which cross federal lands and existed prior to October 21, 1976.

WILDERNESS POLICY

Beaver County, Utah recommends that all future wilderness designations exclude areas containing resources necessary to the economic well-being of the affected local residents. Also, the management of designated wilderness areas must provide for the necessary public access to maintain resources including but not limited to water, minerals, timber, rangeland and intensive recreation uses.

SUSTAINED YIELD - MULTIPLE USE
PRINCIPLES
     Beaver County, Utah is highly dependent upon federal lands, which comprise 14.7 percent of the county land base. It is essential that these federal lands be managed so as to allow appropriate multiple uses. Attempts by narrow interest groups and federal agencies to restrict land uses on federal lands should be reviewed and closely coordinated with affected local governments.
     We hope that these policy statements are a valuable addition to THE WISE USE AGENDA and wish you well in your efforts.

Chad W. Johnson, Chairman
Beaver County Commission

[Editor's Note: The statements of Beaver County and Garfield County, Utah were prepared jointly and contain identical wording. Both are published in full as a matter of courtesy.]

**Northwest Independent
Forest Manufacturers**
Tacoma, Washington

Dear President Bush,

     Please accept the following as Northwest Independent Forest Manufacturers recommendations for THE WISE USE AGENDA.

FOREST SERVICE

No Timber Impact Land Exchange Regulations. The Forest Service should develop land exchange regulations that ensure no exchange will impact the long term sustained yield of national forests containing commercial forest land.

Wise Use of National Forest Timber Receipts. The Congress of the United States should pass a law that permanently directs the Secretary of the Treasury to make available to the Secretary of Agriculture, to remain available until expended, 75% of all National Forest Fund timber receipts received by the Treasury from the harvesting of National Forest Timber. All receipts shall be made available to the Secretary of Agriculture for the following National Forest Systems programs: National Forest trail maintenance and construction; wildlife and fish habitat management; soil, water and air management; cultural resource management; wilderness management; timber sales administration and management; and timber stand improvement activities.

Domestic Processing Policy. Timber from National Forest lands should continue to be made available for processing in the United States. Current regulations which prevent the substitution of National Forest timber for timber exporting from private lands should be strengthened.

Commercial Forest Land Designation. Congress should enact legislation that establishes a National Commercial Timber Harvest System which preserves all suitable commercial forest acres identified in the Final Environmental Impact Statement and Proposed Land and Resource Management Plan for each National Forest.

NATIONAL PARKS AND FOREST SERVICE

"Let Burn" Policy. In forest regions where

there is a need to preserve "old growth" timber as habitat for many species of plants, animals, micro-organisms and recreational and tourism values in our parks and wilderness areas, the National Park Service and U. S. Forest Service shall adopt fire policies that require aggressive suppression of all wildfires; thereby promoting the growth of future "old growth" stands.

Ted J. LaDoux
Director of Forestry Affairs

California Association of Four Wheel Drive Clubs Inc.
Sacramento, California

Dear President Bush,
    There is one subject that we would like to add to your list for the "Agenda for the Wise Use of the Environment". This item deals with the use of motorized vehicles on public lands. As you may already know, Presidential Executive Orders 11644 and 11989, both concern regulation of off road vehicles on public lands. The orders are quite clear relative to how the agencies will apply the intent of the national policy.
    However, the federal agencies that control the affected public lands are not always consistent in their application of these orders. This is largely due to lack of guidance, funding, interest and staff support among the agencies. Off road vehicles can be successfully managed provided the agencies are given the proper tools to do the job. This same philosophy applies to management of all our re-sources.
    The wise use of our resources mandates that we intelligently manage all resource activities, and not sacrifice any one of them for lack of national

direction, planning and funding.

The off road vehicle community is ready to voluntarily support a national gasoline tax program to support this country's needs. We think this is a great idea for the Bush administration to consider.

Ed Dunkley
Field Representative

P.L.U.S. - Public Land Users Society
Tacoma, Washington

Dear President Bush,

The following Wise Use Agenda recommendations are submitted in behalf of the Public Land Users' Society.

NATIONAL PARK SERVICE

Park Management Policies: The National Park Service management policy should place greater emphasis on accommodating the public within the boundaries of national parks.

Management policies should ensure that National Park Service jurisdiction in the area of land use planning be confined within congressionally established national park boundaries.

The national parks should be managed to protect Inholders rights, allow opportunities for rights-of-way to private inholdings and use condemnation procedures only as a last resort.

The national parks should provide for a variety of balanced recreational uses, such as, vehicular sightseeing, bicycling, horseback riding, and hiking.

Boundary Expansion: The Congress of the United States should only permit park expansion where there is a overwhelming benefit to the majority of U.S. Citizens and where administrative boundary adjustments between federal agencies are necessary to improve the overall management of our public lands.

FOREST SERVICE

Wilderness Expansion: Forest Service policy should protect both the Wilderness and the public's right to enjoy the Wilderness by ensuring that use is dispersed in an environmentally sound manner. More trails should be developed throughout the system which are open to hikers, horses and the handicapped. In addition, there should be no further inclusion of Wilderness on national forest lands other than the acres presently classified by Acts of Congress.

Road and Trail System: Congress should enact legislation that creates a National Off-Road Vehicle Trail and Road System that directs the U. S. Forest Service to conduct an in-depth inventory of recreational off-road trail and road uses and opportunities on each national forest, including adjacent land owners. This legislation should further direct the agency to establish and implement a balanced off-road vehicle trail and road system that resolves user conflicts.

Creation of Historic Four Wheel Drive Travel Way: The U. S. Forest Service should aggressively pursue the designation of a historic 4 wheel drive travel way within the Wenatchee and Snoqualmie National Forests as a National Historic 4 Wheel Drive Trail.

Federal Land Exchange and Acquisition: There is a sufficient federal land base to accommodate recreational demands, therefore there should be no need for extensive national forest land exchanges and acquisition.

Public Access: The forest service should allow and encourage access to mining claims as provided by law and should remove unnecessary restrictions and regulations which discourage prospecting and rockhounding. Access to both riparian (streamside) and upland areas is critical.

Increased Demand for Recreational Facilities: The forest service should provide for the enhancement of public enjoyment by taking aggressive action to maintain, reconstruct and develop campgrounds and day use areas.

John Hosford
Co-Chairman

Mountain States Legal Foundation
Denver, Colorado

Dear President Bush,

ECONOMIC USE OF THE PUBLIC LANDS IS A RIGHT OF WESTERN STATES

The public land management agencies, the Department of the Interior and the Department of Agriculture, must recognize that economic use of the public lands is a legitimate and essential part of the status quo of those lands. Timber production, livestock grazing, mineral development, and mining on the public lands means jobs, economic security, and increased state, Federal and local revenues. Time and time gain environmentalists, bureaucrats, and the media use pictures of a logging cut or a mine as examples of environmental degradation and pollution. Such illustrations constitute gross misinformation. These actions are no more detrimental to the environment than the process that results in a field of corn stubble. They are simply evidence of land in production for the benefit of the Nation.

Economic utilization of the public lands is a' right of the Western States. In the early years of the republic, Congress sold lands to those states seeking statehood. Although those sales ended prior to settlement of the West, the legislative histories of most of the statutes governing those western federal lands illustrate that Congress still wanted those lands to be developed for the economic benefit of the West. This right to the economic use of the federal lands is essential to the Western economies. It is their right under the law.

NATIONAL ENVIRONMENTAL POLICY ACT (NEPA)

NEPA should be amended to eliminate any presumption of irreparable injury for purposes of issuance of a preliminary injunctions. Injury to the plaintiff, to the resource developer and to the public should be balanced as they are in the traditional preliminary injunction test. No special judicial favoritism should be given in environmental suits. In no case should an injunction be issued under NEPA where the substantive law mandates that a federal agency approve an action.

NEPA should be amended to provide for a statute of limitations for suits challenging the sufficiency of NEPA documentation. Sixty days after the issuance of a final environmental impact statement (EIS) or a finding of no significant impact (FONSI) is sufficient.

NEPA should be amended to provide for automatic approval of an action where the agency decision is delayed because of federal delays in NEPA compliance. Small projects should be completed in 45 days while larger actions should not exceed one year.

NEPA should be amended to provide for compensation for delay and losses to third parties resulting from environmental lawsuits challenging governmental compliance with NEPA.

NEPA should be amended to make it clean
that future stages of mineral exploration should be
considered in the NEPA review required prior to the
first stages of mineral exploration. No additional
NEPA documentation should ten be necessary following the initial analysis.

Congress should appropriate money for regional environmental studies which are the government's duty under the Federal Land Policy and
Management Act and the National Forest Management Act. Industry should not bear the costs for
federal compliance.

NEPA should be amended to make it clear
that programmatic EIS's need not be completed
except where significant cumulative environmental
impacts can reasonably be alleged.

FEDERAL LAND POLICY AND MANAGEMENT ACT (FLPMA)

Regulations should be adopted requiring
uniform standards for determination of environmental impact under FLPMA's undue degradation
standard, 43 U.S.C. sec. 1732(b), impairment of
suitability standard, 43 U.S.C. sec. 1782(c), and
other similarly vague standards. For example,
standards for approval of mining plans of operation
vary widely between states and in some instances
are granted at the discretion of low level employees
at the Bureau of Land Management (BLM). At the
present time, approval of a mining plan of operations may depend on which BLM employee reviews
it.

THE ENDANGERED SPECIES ACT (ESA)

The ESA should be amended to make it clear
that it may not override the established rights of the
public land users. For example, ESA should not be

used to justify the closure of the only winter access road to a small town.

NATIONAL FOREST MANAGEMENT ACT (NFMA)

Regulations should be adopted to recognize the statutory mandate of multiple use on National Forest lands. Wildlife and other environmental concerns cannot be paramount to the economic uses of the public lands.

Regulations should be adopted to make it clear that the Forest Service has an obligation to offer a continuous supply of timber, sufficient to sustain local economies. Current regulations requiring the Forest Service to plan for the stability of local economies should be strengthened.

Contrary to present policy, the costs of the excessively cumbersome federal decision making process, over-staffing of federal agencies, and excessive environmental measures should not be added to the costs of timber sales to make them appear to be "below cost."

Forest Service planning regulations should be strengthened to require that the allowable sale quantity of timber specified in Forest Service Land and Resource Management Plans be binding. Such a requirement would assist timber companies in planning for future timber supplies.

GENERAL MINING LAW OF 1872

The General Mining Law is a tried and true statute. It has served our nation well, and with the addition of other surface management regulations, also allows for environmental protection. The Mining Law of 1872 should not be repealed or replaced.

GRAZING ON THE PUBLIC LANDS

Legislation should be enacted making it clear that livestock grazing on the public lands is right, not a revocable license or mere privilege. The value of that right should reflect that fact. The fee or cost of that right should be based on the formula established by the Public Rangelands Improvement Act.

Eric Twelker, attorney at law, for
Mountain States Legal Foundation

Mr. and Mrs. John R. Lathrop
Bonney Lake, Washington

Dear President Bush,

As the operators of a small business, our concerns for your administration are as follows:

1. Further "lock-up" of public and private lands and further use restrictions will adversely affect both the free trade economy, and will create a loss of jobs and deny access to special populations, i.e., hunters, fishermen, backpackers and campers, recreational and off-trail vehicle users, and especially the elderly and the physically handicapped. For example, there is a large blind population that skis cross-country who must have road access, facilities, and people who can see to support them, as well as public transportation. Retired persons who fish and camp in small trailers are not the same population who has young legs and lungs and wants more pristine mountains.

2. As our children and grandchildren grow up, we are seeing a decline in decent-paying jobs. The current job growth figures that are quoted do not take into account that the increase in jobs has been in the low-end and minimum wage service industry. Statistics stating that women have gained in wage parity with men don't take into account that men's wages have gone down. That skews the entire women's wage parity data.

3. As a small businessperson, it has been a

nightmare of juggling paperwork, agencies, employee regulations, consumer laws, and so on. I was fortunate to have been able to sell my company in January, 1988, but in December, 1987, I was audited by the Washington State Department of Revenue, the Washington State Department of Labor and Industries (I received refunds in both cases), had a sexual harassment charge filed by a female employee against a male employee and my corporation, and had a three-year-old unattended boy drink a bottle of gas dryer in one of my stores. Small business, the backbone of America's economy, has no organized national lobby. the National Federation of Businessmen and the National Chamber of Commerce are just not interested or effective in responding to the needs of mom and pop businesses or those that employ twenty-five or so persons.

My point is that there are just too many regulations.

We hope the goals of the new administration will be the defense of the free enterprise system. We both believe that growth is not an obscene word, and that intelligent, managed growth is the solution to at least part of the national debt.

Mr. and Mrs. John R. Lathrop

West Coast Alliance for Resources and Environment (WE CARE)
Eureka, California

Dear President Bush,

The West Coast Alliance for Resources and Environment is a community-based, grassroots group that promotes wise management and multiple use for our land and the protection of industry. We are concerned with resource-related issues which affect our lifestyle, both economic and historic. It is this rural lifestyle that we want to enhance and protect.

Currently, W.E. C.A.R.E. represents over 4,500 members and is organized under a "parent" organization, The Alliance for Environment and Resources, which is networked throughout California and the United States.

Sustained supply of timber from public lands (Forest Service, BLM, State, etc.) is a vital part of our timber-dependent communities. In the past twenty years, our resource base has dwindled at the hands of "urban preservationists." This has increased the burden on the Forest Service to supply timber to our resource dependent communities.

On the Six Rivers National Forest, timber receipts totalled over $20 million, of which approximately $5 million was returned to our counties to maintain our high level of education and improve our extensive system of roads. timber sales off the Six Rivers also provided 2,120 jobs. All of this without the need to raise taxes. the government can manage the forests for the good of all and still turn a profit.

With this mind, W.E. C.A.R.E. urges this administration to ensure that our National Forests are managed for "multiple uses" and not just the narrow-minded preferences of a few.

We would like to see the following included in this administration's policy:

● The United States forest Service has the responsibility to the nation to professionally manage the forest for timber production, along with other commodities and amenities.

● The U.S.F.S. has the responsibility to each dependent community to offer an acceptable harvest level based on the biological capability of the forest. Statutory regulation should be sought to reach these goals. Special interest groups should not be allowed to subvert this responsibility.

● Each Forest should be offered an incentive to reach Allowable Sale Quantity.

● This administration should realize that it has the responsibility to ensure that budgetary funding is available to the Forests.

● Society has a continuing demand for lumber and wood by-products. It is the responsibility of any administration to realize that trees are a renewable resource, and that ill-conceived regulations, brought on by special interest groups, can cause the most prudent manager to forego long-range planning.

● The nation and the world should be informed that "nothing is produced from a forest unless you cut a tree."

● The U.S.F.S. should set its policies and goals at the top. There should be a process of accountability to ensure goals are met and policy is adhered to. Too often, non-managers give opinion and the general public takes this to be the position of the entire Forest Service.

● The different governmental agencies should not feel the need to compete with each other for land acquisition. these agencies should see themselves as part of a larger whole. When this is not the case, rural communities find themselves losing more and more of their land base. The designations of land (i.e. wetlands, parks, wilderness, etc.), should be taken as a whole and not as how much each agency, on its own, has. This will lessen the burden on the counties.

● As long as the government continues to buy up land, development of communities will be hindered. the government takes the land that could otherwise be used for mitigation purposes. If this land is not available, the communities suffer.

● We urge support of incentive programs that will encourage private forest landowners, both industrial and non-industrial, to intensify forest management activities on their properties.

● We urge you to reduce the backlog of frivolous appeals in our court system, which cost everyone -- taxpayers, government, landowners -- except those who appeal. We suggest a bond be provided by each appellant so that, in the event the appeal were deemed frivolous, the money can be used to lessen the monetary hardships caused by the appeal.

● We encourage this administration to make the filing of an appeal more difficult by requiring the appellant to prove, beyond a doubt, that he/she/they are personally and seriously affected by the operation that is being appealed.

● Recreation, as it is today, is many times provided for the privileged. Recreation should be made available to the handicapped, young and old. this includes national parks being made accessible to the handicapped.

● Wilderness is not accessible to most people, yet it is considered a recreation area. This misconception should be dispelled.

● The country should be informed that national parks are not the same as state parks or wilderness. The facts about these different land designations should be made known.

● The Wilderness Act of 1984 led us to believe that the final word on wilderness had been said. Now we find ourselves threatened with wilderness again and again. Since this is not the final word, all productive lands that have been removed from the productive land base should come up for periodic review to see if perhaps this designation is not acceptable, and whether it would be in the public interest to place this land back in production.

● Preservation of wildlife is a concern to us all. It is unfortunate that in this decade the true protection and management of wildlife is being overshadowed by the preservationists-obstruction-ists use of wildlife preservation as an excuse to halt timber harvesting. W.E. C.A.R.E. urges your administration to see through these misrepresentations and false allegations of species extinction, and to protect those species that are truly in need.

● We urge the support of private and public fishery enhancement projects through incentive programs.

Rural communities are considered the playground for urbanites who put unreasonable demands on our land base, our economies and our freedom to feed, clothe and shelter ourselves and our families; and to provide the food and fiber to do so for the rest of the nation.

WE ARE THE PEOPLE OF THE REDWOOD HEARTLAND

Those of us who seek out life in this part of rural America live here by choice. Whether we are native sons and daughters who choose to remain and grow where our families' roots have long been planted, or whether we are solace-seekers come to rest in the slower-paced lifestyle of the Redwood Region, we are here by choice.

The country lifestyle is not for everyone. We are content here for reasons and values beyond the need for numbers. These underlying values are commonly articulated amongst ourselves, but not adequately communicated to those in large urban populations.

Our purpose is to articulate these values that make our lifestyle possible and to let people know that the quality of our life is dependent upon productive and wise use of our rural lands.

Americans living in cities have become infatuated with the idea of "wilderness" without realizing the great benefits of perpetuating the culture that exists in rural America. Urban populations little realize that millions of acres in outlying areas have already been set aside and are now unavailable for productive private or productive public use.

We rural Americans value our ability to own, to care for and to utilize land, to work where we live, to be free from government subsidy, and to enhance the quality of our lives through our own initiative. Our culture here is a fragile ecosystem all its own, made up of hard-working people and the land, an inter-relationship which provides food and fiber for the rest of the country.

However, this quality of rural life that binds us to the north coast is far more than the products it creates.

This is a culture that recognizes that people are a prime part of nature, not alien to it, and that mankind can live and work symbiotically here, using his creative intelligence as nature's crowning touch.

The threat of further land withdrawals that impact the quality and the economic condition of our lifestyles and our culture rouses us to action. We believe our cultural heritage is worth protecting and maintaining, and in order to accomplish this, we will work diligently to communicate the following ideas and concepts upon which our lifestyle is based:

1. Broad expansive forests that are creatively managed for timber production can provide the solitude, aesthetic beauty, wildlife habitat, grasslands and clean water commonly associated with the "wilderness experience."

2. Many lands that visitors to our area see and enjoy as "open space" are actually productive, well-managed agricultural lands that enhance the appeal of rural country.

3. Nature originally revitalized the forests and the atmosphere by creating new growth through forest fires. Young, growing trees convert more

carbon dioxide to oxygen than do old, decadent forests. When a mature forest was destroyed by fire, natural regeneration occurred through successive stages, creating diverse habitats and other environmental benefits. man has improved upon this natural process through creative, active forest management on a sustained yield basis. Today, seven to ten trees of superior genetic qualities are planted for every tree harvested. Varied species ensure the quality of successive generations in the forests.

4. We have already set aside many millions of acres in California (and the rest of the U.S.) that will not be used to produce food, fiber or jobs, and that are off-limits to most types of recreational uses. Therefore, additional acres of wilderness, access to which humans will be denied, are unnecessary and have a negative effect on our quality of life.

5. People are a part of nature. Those who utilize the land need not be thought of as detracting from its beauty or value. This is not a case of environment versus business, because the careful husbanding of the land enhances resources for generations to come.

6. A reasonable balance between productive lands and non-productive lands must be maintained if we are to preserve the rural culture that makes the "country" a nice place to visit. The human habitat in rural America is as fragile (and economically tenuous) as that of any endangered species.

7. The public is often most benefited by private ownership and utilization of rural lands, as opposed to publicly-controlled land management. Rather than creating wilderness just for the sake of wilderness, to assuage the noble aspirations of preservationists, existing state and federal park and wilderness lands should be enhanced and developed to encourage their use by all Americans

desiring the "wilderness experience."

OBJECTIVES

1. Maintain a productive land base for the production of food and fiber.

2. Serve the public interest by sustaining the private sector's ability to provide agricultural and forest products at affordable prices.

3. Emphasize that land in private ownership is more efficiently managed than land in public ownership, regardless management goals.

4. Encourage state and federal governments to maintain, improve and develop existing public lands before considering additions to the public land base.

5. Assert that the right to manage private lands should be maintained without the unnecessary restrictions that might arise from nearby public land acquisition.

6. Insist that a complete environmental and economic impact report be prepared for any proposed acquisition of private lands by the government.

7. Oppose government meeting the desires of special interest groups by means of private land acquisition to the detriment of private landowners, the local economy and local government.

8. Oppose erosion of the local tax base.

9. Oppose the extension of state and federal condemnation and eminent domain powers.

The United States Forest Service has the responsibility to the nation to professionally manage the forest for timber production, along with other commodities and amenities.

The Forest Service has the responsibility to

each dependent community to offer an acceptable harvest level based on the biological capability of the forest. Statutory regulation should be sought to reach these goals. Special interest groups should not be allowed to subvert this responsibility.

Liz Tomascheski-Adams
Executive Coordinator

North West Timber Association
Eugene, Oregon

Dear President Bush,

In many parts of the west the continued economic and social stability of communities is dependent upon a reasonable and stable timber supply from dominant Forest Service and Bureau of Land Management lands. Over the past two decades legislative actions (Wilderness, National Park expansions, Wild and Scenic Rivers, etc.) have steadily reduced the timber landbase and thus the sustainable timber supply, causing reduced economic activity and higher consumer prices for wood products. Congressionally directed planning (NFMA, FLPMA) and legal hurdles (NEPA) have further increased the instability of our communities as wildlife, water, non-road recreation and visual management have been emphasized while community stability has been relegated to a residual position to be considered only after all other values are accommodated.

The portion of the public land base available for commodity production must be stabilized and protected much as areas have been reserved for non-timber use such as Wilderness.

A minimum level of timber and other commodity outputs necessary to stabilize and maintain the public timber dependent communities should be identified for each unit of the national forests. Minimum output requirements must be established by law.

Dennis Hayward
Executive Vice President

National Inholders Association
Washington, D.C. and Sonoma, California

Dear President Bush,
  An inholder is an owner of private property interests within government lands, which may include owners of real estate, cabin permits, grazing permits, timber contracts and other valuable private property rights. The National Inholders Association represents inholders to Congress and other forums to protect their rights.
  The people of the Wise Use Movement are themselves a valuable resource that should not be dismissed lightly. Their life on the land, their natural wisdom and their productivity all give depth and shape to the meaning of America. Far from being a threat to the land as extremists portray them, these diligent and dedicated people are good stewards who increase the natural gift of productivity in our nation through wise use and sound conservation practices.
  Socially, the people of the Wise Use Movement are a priceless asset teaching our affluent society the forgotten value of basic economic commodity production, industriousness, foresight and endurance in the face of overwhelming obstacles, both natural and manmade.

INHOLDERS AS AN ASSET-PARTNERS IN OUT-DOOR RECREATION
  The Problem: Resource managers have been

taught that inholders are a threat to recreation areas and should be removed. This concept has become policy in most federal agencies. It has turned supporters into adversaries. The result is constant bureaucratic pressure against inholders, more land acquisition than necessary, higher costs, loss of volunteer stewardship, and the loss of unique rural cultures which add to the visitor experience.

The Solution: Co-Management. Make inholders an asset. Involve them in land planning and turn them into allies. The country cannot afford to buy out all the nice places that need protection. Private stewardship, in cooperation with land planning agencies, is the answer. It would reduce land protection costs through the use of easements and alternatives and make landowners part of the solution instead of enemies. The English and French systems provide successful examples.

Inholders, again, are people who own land or other equity interests such as grazing permits, recreation cabins, mining claims, and water rights within the boundaries of federally managed areas, or who are impacted by the management, regulation of, or access to those areas. Over one million people are inholders.

They own: land in National Parks, private land, recreation permits, special use permits, grazing permits and other rights in National Forests and areas managed by the Bureau of Land Management. They include a variety of privately owned uses in areas managed by the Fish and Wildlife Service, Corps of Engineers, and Bureau of Reclamation.

When Congress creates a federally designated area, there is generally considerable public support by residents and those living on adjacent lands. However, the record shows, as in Cuyahoga

Valley, that the promises made to them to gain their support are often broken.

The traditional federal method for dealing with conflicts, real or perceived, between private ownership, federal management and recreation objectives has been to remove the private interest.

Gradually, private users that are promised the ability to continue are driven from the scene. Often, recreation opportunities are also driven out. Landowners and others begin to fight any federal involvement because of this trend and the result is less recreation, not more.

A variety of methods are used by the federal agencies to gain control. The use of condemnation or eminent domain to acquire private land, homes and farms has had a devastating impact on the rural culture of America. Numerous films, television shows, magazine and newspaper articles document the abuses.

Regulation of inholders is also an enormous problem. The federal agency gradually takes over an area designated for special management through an ever-increasing series of regulations. Private uses and access are reduced. It becomes uneconomic for private interests to continue. Co-management of these areas could change this.

Secretary of the Interior Donald Hodel was quoted in the "Daily Oklahoman," Friday, December 6, 1985, about the proposed Tallgrass Prairie Preserve: "Any obstacle to drilling or grazing would depend on the legislation that creates the park. But there is a trap in that. If legislation says grazing and drilling is permitted, as soon as the park is created, there will be an enormous push to prevent it by banning it outright or raising so much red tape that it could become impossible. Like night follows day, it's an unwavering principle of park development. There's a constituency that would oppose any development. Within five years, anyone carrying on

commercial activity in the park would find it difficult if not impossible to operate."

By treating inholders or private interests as
allies in the effort to expand recreation, a wide vista
of new opportunities would come into focus. Private
investment, secure with long-term leases and a
friendly neighbor in the federal government, would
increase.

Inholders who are already there, and who
own portions of the checkerboarded lands inter-
mixed with federal land, can provide the best and
least expensive way to expand recreation if they are
brought into the process and treated fairly.

FOREST RECREATION CABINS THREATENED BY AGENCY POLICY

The Problem: Forest Service recreation residence program is under threat of gradual phaseout.
Poor appraisals and high fees could make cabin
sites only available to rich. Agency termination
policy has led to the loss of hundreds of cabins and
loss of morale. 1,300 tract and isolated cabins are
under termination.

The Solution: Recognize recreation residences
as a valuable part of multiple use in the forests. they
provide the highest income per acre of any recreation use in the forests and allow access and a
valuable recreation experience for many people who
otherwise might not be able to use the forests. This
is especially true for the handicapped, elderly and
children. Cabin owners are stewards of the forests
who provide many valuable services. Private investment by permittees often makes up for the lack
of federal funding.

Ever since the 1962 Outdoor Recreation
Resources Review Commission there has been an
unwritten Forest Service policy to gradually eliminate the 16,800 "recreation residences" and "isolated cabins" by the year 2000. This has led to years

of conflict between permittees and the agency which damaged a previously successful program and partnership.

The agency is presently terminating 1,300 "recreation residences" and "isolated cabins." Present policy is to remove all isolated cabin uses. This policy is costly, brings many appeals, and leads to the loss of a valuable human resource that could help make up for agency funding shortfalls through private investment in roads, fire protection, and other services.

Poor appraisals and uneven application of appraisal standards has led to large variations in permit fees. Permittees in Priest Lake, Idaho have been paying fees in excess of $2,000, and as high as $6,000, for a single lot for one year. State tracts at the same lake pay a fraction of the cost. In other areas of the country, a similar lot is charged only $150 a year.

Many cabin sites in existing tracts are unfilled due to present policies. These sites could provide recreation to thousands of families and others who use their facilities.

The Forest Service has failed to recognize permittees as assets. Gradually, many permittees have been turned from friends into enemies.

Agency policy must be changed to encourage the recreation residence program to continue. Fees must be fair and equitable to prevent cabins from being only available to the rich. Agency personnel should be encouraged to look at the benefits of recreation cabins, both in tracts and in isolated areas, and take advantage of the private stewardship and cost benefits possible with a better relationship with permittees.

GRAZING SUBSIDIZES RECREATION -- STOCKMEN'S RIGHTS MUST BE RECOGNIZED

The Problem: Grazing is a long-term, legally

established economic use of the federal lands. Grazing rights and water rights are privately owned property rights. Agencies and some special interest groups are attempting to take these rights or legislate grazing out of existence. The resulting threat is causing stockmen, normally friends of recreation, to close access to private land as well as public land where access requires going through private land for recreational purposes.

The Solution: Grazing must be recognized as an activity that subsidizes recreation. The investments by stockmen in grazing permits, water development and range improvements on federal land help wildlife and subsidize recreation. These investments must be recognized and compensated, or traded for, when a conflict over recreation develops.

Continuous attempts have been made to eliminate grazing from federal areas with the idea that it is an activity that conflicts with public purposes and diminishes recreational opportunities.

In reality, stockmen invest large sums of money in roads, fences, and water improvements that enhance wildlife propagation. This advances and subsidizes such recreation as fishing and hunting. Failure to acknowledge the existence of privately held water, grazing, and range rights, and the possessory interest in federal land they generate, has led to unending conflict.

The solution is to recognize grazing and water rights as private property rights. In addition, we should acknowledge the economic benefits other segments of society receive from privately funded range improvements.

Efforts have been made by the federal agencies, as well as special interest groups, to regulate out of existence, or legislate the removal of grazing without recognition of or compensation for the huge investment by most stockmen in range improvements. These activities are gradually turning stockmen away from their traditional support for recreation activities.

In large areas of grazing land managed by the Bureau of Land Management and Forest Service, there is so much private investment and so many private rights, that the area is actually not public land, but split estate land, with the stockmen owning a significant percentage of the bundle of rights to the land.

In some cases, the percentage owned by the stockmen is so large, and the government's percentage so small, that the land title should be conveyed to cut management costs and get land on the tax rolls.

Recreation conflict resolution and allocation of recreation resources would be easier if the investments by stockmen were recognized and they were compensated for their economic loss in the event of a conflict over a recreation use.

Grazing should be recognized as a positive contribution to recreation.

LAND AND WATER CONSERVATION FUND TOOL FOR ABUSE

The Problem: The LWCF has become a tool for some special interests to destroy the fabric of rural communities and reduce recreational opportunities for large segments of society at unnecessary cost to the taxpayers.

The Solution: Any future fund of this type must have tight controls and effective and continuous oversight. the new direction must be to purchase only sufficient interests in lands necessary to meet the intent of Congress for the area.

According to the General Accounting Office, to a large extent, no effective priority system has been used with this fund. Lands have been purchased in fee title without considering the need for such purchases, alternatives to fee acquisition or cost-effectiveness of such purchases.

For too many years, the federal government has supported the philosophy that we need to buy in fee as much land as possible within dedicated boundaries regardless of: (1) cost; (2) whether the purchase is necessary; (3) whether alternatives exist; (4) the rights of the landowners; and (5) the socio-cultural effects of large-scale purchases of land on local communities and land use patterns.

Robert Herbst, former Assistant Secretary for Fish, Wildlife and Parks described the result at the 1980 National Park Service Advisory Board meeting as a land acquisition backlog exceeding three billion dollars. Others have suggested that the figure may be much higher.

Each federal project must have a limited amount of funding for fee title purchases for public use areas with adequate provisions for alternatives. Each federal area should have an approved Land Protection Plan along with a General Management Plan prior to beginning acquisition. Priorities should be established after full public participation. Only the interests necessary to manage the area and meet the intent of Congress should be purchased.

LAND PROTECTION PLANS -- IMPLEMENTATION NEEDED

The Problem: The Department of Interior created the Land Protection Planning Process for the purpose of protecting more land at less cost, but plans have not been effectively implemented to meet that purpose.

The Solution: Land Protection Plans should be rewritten where Department purpose and intent has not been achieved.

The Land Protection Planning process is one of the most innovative and necessary programs to be initiated in this decade. It is a logical approach to the broad question of "what are we buying, and at what cost?"

Land Protection Plans both identify the land and degrees of title to the land needed by the federal government to protect the resource and designate cost-effective alternatives to full federal purchase, such as easements.

During times of severe fiscal constraints, this approach is even more valid. Aside from the issue of social and cultural disruption associated with large-scale acquisition of lands, our government can no longer afford to buy lands at the same rate as the last 20 years. We must begin to determine how much is enough.

The General Accounting Office, in their report GAO/RCED-86-16 dated October 31, 1985, "New Rules For Protecting Land in the National park System -- Consistent Compliance Needed," "found that 25 of 38 Land Protection Plans it reviewed did not implement Interior policy or comply with National Park Service rules."

"If the Park Service implements the plans' recommendations that do not comply with its rules, it could acquire more interest in land than it needs, incur unnecessary acquisition costs, and deplete the limited funds available for land protection."

The Land Protection concept should be revived with the idea of achieving the purpose for which it was intended.

CONGRESSIONAL INTENT AND LEGISLATIVE HISTORIES IGNORED BY FEDERAL AGENCIES

The Problem: Both the Forest Service and Park Service have ignored the intent of Congress while implementing new park and recreation areas. While Congress intended more public use in some areas, the Park Service manages all areas the same way. The results have been: far more land acquisition than anticipated by Congress; greater costs; and almost no use of alternative means of land protection. As a result, local land owners and communities have turned against federal recreation schemes.

The Solution: A clear understanding of the intent of Congress by the federal agency before it begins to develop new parks and recreation areas. Require all land planning, acquisition and management personnel to read and be familiar with all legislative histories for their areas. Require land protection plans in each area before acquisition begins.

The General Accounting Office, the investigative arm of Congress, has been extremely critical of federal land acquisition programs, particularly those of the Park Service. It suggested in a series of recent reports that the Park Service had gone so far beyond congressional intent, that it should sell much of the land it purchased back to the original owners because it was not needed.

The GAO suggested that the Park Service managed most of its areas the same way, regardless of congressional priorities. Examples:

● Lake Chelan National Recreation Area -- GAO said that Park Service land acquisition had actually cut overnight lodging in half. Other Park Service actions cut available recreation activities. Far more land was acquired than was intended by Congress. This turning point report recommended that the agency sell the land back to private owners.

● Buffalo River -- Land acquisition destroyed the unique farming culture that existed along the river. Almost no easements were used, although they were recommended by Congress. The Park Service is now trying to re-establish the culture and rent the farms back to private owners, yet is continuing to make the same mistakes in other areas.

● St. Croix River -- GAO found in 1978 that the Park Service had purchased over 21,000 acres when they were only supposed to buy 1,000. Again, in 1979, GAO found more people facing condemnation than the agency was legally able to condemn. The State of Minnesota was able to protect as much land as the Park Service, but for far less cost, using easements.

● Mt. Rogers NRA -- In 1980 the Forest Service published a master plan indicating many more condemnations. A review of the legislative history showed that Congress specified 39,500 acres as the amount of land to purchase, 40% in scenic easements. At that time the agency had purchased 26,000 acres in fee with no easements. After intervention by the local congressman, the Forest Service curtailed their plans.

● Many other examples exist. In one recent report, the GAO only found one area out of 21 examined where the agency was managing it consistent with the intent of Congress.

Each agency should be required to have a complete copy of the legislative history, including congressional debates, House and Senate Committee Reports, Conference Reports and other important documents in the park or recreation area. All personnel associated with management, planning, and land acquisition should be required to be familiar with this information. Other oversight procedures should be set up to make sure the agency is obeying the law . . . and the intent of Congress.

LOCAL PLANNING FOR FEDERAL AREAS: OPPORTUNITIES FOR SUBSTANTIAL SAVINGS AND BETTER COMMUNITY RELATIONS

The Problem: Only federal alternatives have been considered in the planning of federally-managed areas, resulting in unnecessary project delays, insufficient state and local input, unnecessary conflict, controversy, and frequent departure from legislative intent.

The Solution: Federal funds, on a matching

basis when appropriate, should be provided to state and local governments for the planning of federal areas in conjunction with the appropriate agency.

The "Beltway Syndrome" has been too evident in the planning of federal areas in the past. Often times those doing the planning, whether in Washington or the Denver Service Center, do not have adequate familiarity with the resource, and the management plan becomes unacceptable. The result is local opposition and unneeded delays and costs.

There are alternatives that really work. by capturing strong local support, land protection becomes easier and cheaper. These areas are often significant components of the economies of local government as well as entire states. When local people are involved they can help secure state and federal money. State side financial support continues to be reasonably strong.

The Upper Delaware River is an excellent example of a planning process gone awry, with millions of dollars wasted, costly delays and bitter feelings created among the affected communities.

Enlightened federal management then began working with local government to do a new plan with a real public involvement process. The plan is nearing a successful and community supported conclusion.

The federal cost was $2,000,000 over six years. The local plan, through the Council of Upper Delaware Townships, will cost $500,000 and took two years.

The local plan had to overcome community anger resulting from the federal plan in order to be successful. If local planning had been considered from the start, it probably could have been completed even faster and with less cost.

STATE COMMISSIONS TO MONITOR FEDERAL

AREAS -- A PROVEN NEW IDEA

The Problem: Federal land management agencies, in most cases, have been allowed to operate without sufficient oversight or input at the state or local level.

The Solution: States should consider the establishment of independent commissions or committees to work as partners with the appropriate federal agencies. This is being done successfully in Minnesota and Alaska.

There has been unnecessary conflict and tension in federal recreation projects due to insufficient involvement by state and local governments. Although many national parks and other federal areas have advisory committees, they are in most cases appointed, in effect, by the local park superintendent or land manager. These groups do not provide the kind of balance necessary to provide proper oversight, nor can they be considered truly independent.

Minnesota (in 1975) and Alaska (in 1981) established independent state commissions to work with federal land management agencies. These commissions have balanced representation and professional staff who work with federal officials to resolve conflicts and problems before they become unmanageable.

They work as a conduit for information from the federal agencies to state and local government, as well as local citizen groups. They also act on behalf of citizens to carry their concerns to the federal agency.

The oversight provided by these commissions' professional staffs associated with theses commissions has prevented major problems and forced the federal agencies to operate more consistently with the law, intent of Congress and the needs of state citizens.

A real partnership in management evolves

when the federal agency is not able to simply ignore local input but must coordinate with state and local agencies who have the staff capable of monitoring their activities.

In this way, recreation and resource management benefits. Substantial cost savings result from reduced tension between interest groups. There is far less resentment against the federal agency since state citizens feel they have a place to go for help.

The Commission should recommend that this type of state commission be created in every state to help coordinate efforts to expand recreation opportunities, while mitigating conflicts between citizens and federal agencies.

RECREATION ACCESS FOR THE HANDICAPPED, ELDERLY AND CHILDREN

The Problem: Many federal land management agencies cater to the interests of a small segment of the public who have the time, interest, and physical capacity to engage in limited recreational uses, such as backpacking or strenuous hiking.

The Solution: Federal agency plans and policies should reflect proper consideration of all recreational uses consistent with the legislative intent of the federal area.

National Parks and other federally managed areas appeal to a large number of recreational interests in America. Land managers and federal agencies should recognize and provide for the legitimate needs of all user groups, including the elderly, handicapped and children.

Many land managers have developed a bias for certain uses or user groups over others. This bias leads to bitter feelings between various user groups and often results in management plans and policies that conflict with the legislative intent of the federal area.

Recent trends indicate the need for long term management flexibility. America's population is getting older. We are likely to be less oriented toward Wilderness and more likely to use recreational vehicles.

There are current efforts to establish recreation ares by promising benefits for the whole population. After designation, the agencies and others rush to limit use and development.

Voyageurs National Park is a classic example of promises made and a clear legislative history that made recreation a high priority. Management by the Park Service since then has downplayed recreation and public use, while stressing preservation.

Lake Chelan National Recreation Area is another example where the legislative history favoring recreation was ignored in favor of preservation. Since the creation of the Lake Chelan NRA, the facilities available for overnight accommodations and recreation in Lake Chelan have been cut to less than half. The General Accounting Office soundly criticized Park Service management at Lake Chelan as not following the intent of Congress.

All legitimate interests can be accommodated in most areas if balanced distribution of use, based on demand, is considered and reflected in agency plans and policies. This will require an honest assessment of visitor use statistics and the true meaning of the demands indicated. All segments of society can share in the use of our recreational resources if balanced decisions are made regarding the allocation of those resources consistent with protecting the resource for the future.

Charles S. Cushman
Executive Director

Wilderness Impact Research Foundation
Elko, Nevada

Dear President Bush,

The central theme of the Wilderness Impact Research Foundation is that no further Wilderness should be designated until the impact of the existing 90 million acres has been thoroughly assessed. Excessive Wilderness designation has wrought havoc in the fabric of American industry, economy, popular recreation and our society's vision. No further Wilderness designations should be made by Congress without the specific approval of the legislature of the state in which such designation is being considered. The Foundation specifically supports the people of the Wise Use Movement in their efforts to assess and redirect harmful Wilderness encroachment upon their livelihoods and way of life.

Grant Gerber
Director

Willamette Forestry Council
Creswell, Oregon

Dear President Bush:

The Willamette Forestry Council is composed of dozens of manufacturers, industry associations and private individuals who have joined in an effort to maintain access to material supplies managed by Federal agencies. It is on behalf of the working people of Oregon that the Willamette Forestry Council is writing to you. The Willamette National Forest, last year, produced ten percent of all the revenues in the national timber sale program.

Of all the states, Oregon is first in the production of softwood saw timber for home building, industry and secondary wood products manufacturing. Oregon accounts for one fourth of all the softwood sawtimber grown and used in the United States. Without question, Oregon is "the Nation's Woodbasket."

The Oregon Wood Products Industry provides much more than wood for the needs of the Nation, jobs for industry workers and income for Oregon's Schools and Roads. It provides the economic lifeblood of a state. Over 75,000 workers depend on the Wood Products Industry, the largest employment sector in Oregon. Wood products manufacturing accounts for over $7 billion in annual income to the people of Oregon.

Presently, Timber Supply in Oregon has gained national attention. Most of the forestland in Oregon (60 percent) is in Federal ownership. The National Forest system and lands administered by the Bureau of Land Management provide the bulk of log supply available to the Wood Products industry today. Because this is so, much of the decision-making authority about the economic future or Oregon is concentrated in the hands of federal administrators in the US Forest Service and the Bureau of Land Management.

Although these agencies have done an excellent job of managing the Nation's forest resources in Oregon, they are increasingly under siege by those who have no understanding of the practice of forestry, no comprehension of the renewability of the resource and no concern about the importance of the Wood Products Industry to Oregon and to the Nation.

A multi-million dollar alliance of wilderness associations, preservationist groups and animal rights activists have targeted the Oregon Wood Products Industry for extinction. The theme of their attack -- the preservation of America's last remaining "ancient forests" -- has become an incredibly lucrative fundraising device which has funded legal appeals responsible for eliminating one-third of the log supply coming from forest lands managed by the Bureau of Land Management, and forced delays, withdrawals and cancellations of hundreds of timber sales on other federally-managed lands in Oregon. Mill closures in Oregon are now a weekly event as the Wood Products Industry is being strangled by the timber sale appeals, red tape and legal challenges.

Oregon has already set aside 2.1 million acres, much in primeval forest, in 36 Wilderness areas within the state. These Wilderness Areas provide habitat for Old-Growth dependent species, for primitive recreation opportunities and to maintain a viable gene pool for research and future propagation.

Oregon has enough ancient forest preserved for the future. We now need your help in preserving our working forests for the benefit of all Americans. Please help us maintain the viability of the Wood Products Industry in Oregon so that we may continue to make our contribution to the national economy and the quality of life of our Nation's citizens.

Please remember ... *OREGON! The Nation's Woodbasket.*

Mark Fleming
Chairman

Center for the Defense of Free Enterprise
Bellevue, Washington

Dear President Bush,

The Center is a non-profit, tax exempt educational foundation devoted to protecting the freedom of Americans to enter the marketplace of commerce and the marketplace of ideas without undue government restriction.

In assembling the Wise Use Agenda recommendations placed in your hands through this book, the Center has had occasion to reflect upon the disparity between the huge power of environmentalist organizations in shaping policy and the relative weakness of commodity resource users. We find that the single primary source of this disparity of influence lies in the fact that environmental organizations have thought in *systems*, particularly the vast land-control *systems* on our federal estate -- the National Wilderness Preservation System, the National Wild and Scenic River System, the National Trails System, to name but a few -- while commodity resource users have thought only in specific uses in specific places: there is no balancing set of commodity resource *systems* designated in the federal lands.

There is no National Timber Harvest System, no National Mining System, no National Rangeland Grazing System, no National Petroleum Production System, and no National Off-Road Vehicle Recreation System. Not a single acre of the public domain is devoted officially to these commodity and active recreation uses, and yet vast quantities of our accessible domestic oil and natural gas, renewable timber and grazing forage, fuel and non-fuel minerals and space for active recreation exist on the federal lands, capable of proper management with minimal disturbance to the environment.

As a direct result of this lack of productive commodity systems, these important uses, all of them proper facets of the Multiple Use concept, are increasingly shoved aside by the incursions of endlessly expanding preservation systems. In every place where commodity use has been the traditional historic use of the federal lands, commodity production and active use is being relegated to the left-over lands remaining after all other designations have been satisfied. This is a serious injustice to millions of productive Americans who aspire to contribute to our nation's economic strength.

This has resulted in a dangerous reduction in the productivity of our federal lands, which can potentially be managed for both preservation and use, but which are increasingly managed solely for preservation with commodity use forbidden. Uncertainties over the encroachment of wilderness, wild and scenic rivers, national park expansion and other "systemic cancers" have caused a massive capital flight from potentially productive federal lands: timber harvesting and other commodity uses have vanished from Oregon and Washington and many Western states in massive acreages solely because there is no way an entrepreneur can rely on federal policy to protect the timber, mining, grazing or petroleum commodity use of any federal lands. Hundreds of thousands of loggers, miners, cattlemen and petroleum workers have lost good jobs through flawed federal preservation policy.

Thousands of Americans have been pushed out of their homes to make way for additions to the National Park System near urban areas where "National Recreation Areas" have proliferated. The loss to our economy in opportunity costs now ranges in the hundreds of billions of dollars. The loss to our cherished values of personal independence, private property as the bulwark of individual initiative, and limited government is incalculable and horrendous. All commodity use of the federal lands is under attack and will vanish completely within only a few years unless a National Commodity Use System of federal lands is designated and protected immediately. This is a crisis of unimaginable proportions.

Moreover, these economic losses and the injustice of federal policy has generated a reservoir of angry Americans who have been radicalized by being pushed out of traditional homes and employment through ever-expanding preservationist designations. This subculture of the dispossessed productive citizen poses a serious social threat to the very fabric of American life. Should some unscrupulous charismatic leader with utopian promises arise to exploit the wrongs committed by federal policy, serious disorders could not be far behind. We can save ourselves a harrowing potential revolt and do justice to good people in a single stroke: create the needed federal land system designations to protect commodity uses forever.

The overall National Commodity Use System should be comprised at first of the National Timber Harvest System, the National Mining System, the National Rangeland Grazing System, the National Petroleum Production System, and the National Off-Road Vehicle Recreation System. At a later time, additional commodity use systems may be enacted. Congress should attend to this matter without delay. A model bill for a National Rangeland Grazing System submitted by the National Conference on Federal Lands is included below as an example of what is intended.

We wish you and your Administration all success and urge you to "Think Systems" -- National Commodity Use Systems for the federal lands.

Ron Arnold
Executive Director

National Conference on Federal Lands
Las Vegas, Nevada

Dear President Bush,
        We are pleased to submit our recommendation for wise use of the environment in the form of a draft model bill for a National Rangeland Grazing

System. The model bill is for discussion only and not meant for introduction in Congress without close conference with the relevant commodity interests.

A BILL

Be it enacted by the Senate and House of Representatives of the United States of America in Congress assembled:

Sec. 1. That this Act may be cited as the "National Rangeland Grazing System Act of 1989."

Sec. 2. (a) In order to assure that an increasing urban population, accompanied by expanding disposable income and growing leisure time, does not infringe all rural areas within the United States and its possessions for the purpose of nature preservation, leaving no lands designated for commodity use and productive resource purposes, it is hereby declared to be the policy of the Congress to secure for the American people of present and future generations the benefits of an enduring resource of grazing rangelands. For this purpose there is hereby established a National Rangeland Grazing System to be composed of federally owned areas designated by Congress as "grazing areas", and these shall be administered for the commodity benefit of the American people in such manner as will leave them unimpaired for future use and employment as grazing lands, and so as to provide for the productive use of these areas, the preservation of their productive character, and for the gathering and dissemination of information regarding their use and employment as grazing lands; and no Federal lands shall be designated as "grazing lands" except as provided for in this Act or by a subsequent Act.

(b) The inclusion of an area in the National Rangeland Grazing System notwithstanding, the area shall continue to be managed by the Department and agency having jurisdiction thereover immediately before its inclusion in the National Rangeland Grazing System unless otherwise provided by Act of Congress. No appropriation shall be available for the payment of expenses or salaries for the administration of the National Rangeland Grazing System as a separate unit nor shall any appropriations be available for additional personnel stated as being required solely for the purpose of managing or administering areas solely because they are included within the National Rangeland Grazing System.

(c) A rangeland grazing area, in contrast with those areas where urban development or nature preservation dominate the landscape, is hereby recognized as an area where the land and its ecological conditions are suited to the grazing of livestock, where grazing is the historic use, where preservationists are visitors who do not remain. An area of grazing is further defined to mean in this Act an area of Federal land presently under permit according to the terms of the Taylor Grazing Act [43 U.S.C. 315-315(o)], or managed as rangeland under the Federal Land Policy and Management Act of 1976 [43 U.S.C. 1701-1782] or other applicable rangeland statute, and which (1) generally contains split estate values of privately owned possessory interests in the Federal lands, including but not limited to: water rights, range rights, privately owned range improvements such as roads, fences, stock watering facilities, ranch houses, cook houses, and bunk houses, (2) is rendered more valuable by the contribution of commensurable private land, (3) is biologically suited to grazing by either intensive or extensive livestock management methods, and (4) may also be available to multiple use for purposes including but not limited to hunting, hiking, motorized recreation, watershed management, wildlife management, timber harvest and minerals man-

agement but no application shall impair the operation of the rangeland as livestock grazing areas.

Sec. 3. (a) All areas within the jurisdiction of
the Department of the Interior and the Department
of Agriculture under permit according to the terms
of the Taylor Grazing Act or classified as rangeland
according to applicable statute at least 30 days
before the effective date of this Act are hereby
designated as grazing areas. The Secretary of
Agriculture and the Secretary of the Interior shall --

(1) Inventory. Within five years after the
enactment of this Act, obtain from grazing permittees on the National Rangeland Grazing System an
inventory of all possessory interests in the Federal
lands under their permit.

(2) Evaluate Possessory Interests. Evaluate
the possessory interests of each grazing permittee
using as a basis the evaluation placed by commercial banks or the Internal Revenue Service upon the
permit in estate tax settlements and maintain records of the evaluation of the private possessory
interests in the Federal lands, available to the
public.

(3) Designate Grazing Enterprise Zones.
Where any possessory interests in the Federal lands
are identified by grazing permittees under their
permit, designate such lands as split estate lands.
Where the permittee's possessory interests comprise less than fifty percent of the value of the total
split estate of his permit lands, the Secretaries shall
designate such areas as rangeland enterprise zones
of the National Rangeland Grazing System and
promulgate regulations for joint management of
such enterprise zones, giving due respect to the
possessory interests of the permittee while protecting the majority Federal values in the National
Rangeland Grazing System. Enterprise zone permittees shall be included in Land Use Planning and
Management decision making functions as equal

members of Interdisciplinary Teams (IDTs).

(4) Transfer of Lands. Transfer those lands with more than fifty percent of the split estate values in private ownership to the owner or owners of the values when requested by the owner or owners. In cases where the private owner or owners of a majority interest in the split estate do not wish to accept transfer of those lands, said owner or owners may elect to have the lands designated as Rangeland Enterprise Zones to be managed as in Sec 3. (3) above.

(5) Protected Water Rights. Make no application to any state for stock watering rights on National Rangeland Grazing System lands. Where agency beneficial use can be shown such as campsite watering, the Secretaries may apply for water rights.

(b) The Secretary of Agriculture and the Secretary of the Interior shall, within ten years after the enactment of this Act, review all grazing permits under their jurisdiction to determine whether such permit has been traded in a market since its original grant. Where a grazing permit has been traded and a market value established, the permit shall be designated a valuable private property right of the permittee, which shall not be taken for public use. The United States specifically vacates its power of eminent domain over lands covered by a grazing permit with an established market value.

(c) Within ten years of the effective date of this Act the Secretary of the Interior and the Secretary of Agriculture shall review every grassland area in the Federal lands under his jurisdiction and shall report to the President his recommendation of the suitability or nonsuitability of each such area for inclusion as grazing land. The President shall advise the President of the Senate and the Speaker of the House of Representatives of his recommendation with respect to the designation as grazing areas each such area on which review has been completed, together with a map thereof and a definition of its boundaries. A recommendation of the President shall become effective only if so provided by an Act of Congress.

Sec. 4. Land Use Planning in the National Rangeland Grazing System. As an integrated and equal consideration in developing, maintaining and revising land use plans for the National Rangeland Grazing System pursuant to this Act and the Federal Land Policy and Management Act of 1976, and land and resource management plans for the National Forest System pursuant to the Forest and Rangeland Renewable Resources Planning Act of 1974 as amended by the National Forest Management Act of 1976, the Secretaries of the Interior and Agriculture, respectively, shall in addition to, and in conjunction with, their other integrated planning requirements and responsibilities:

(a) Consider privately owned possessory interests in the federal lands, including but not limited to water rights, range rights, and privately owned range improvements, and the contribution of commensurable private land to federal range values.

(b) Protect all private values of the National Rangeland Grazing System split estate from incursion by nongrazing designations. Grazing is declared to be the dominant use among the many multiple uses in the National Rangeland Grazing System. Such values as riparian habitat, wild horses and burros, where the water rights and grazing rights are privately owned, shall be protected by management plans subject to the advice and approval of the private owner. Damage to forage caused by wildlife, wild horses and burros or recreationists in areas covered by a valid grazing right shall be repaired by the administering agency or compensated by the United States to the rancher.

No privately owned water shall be fenced by any federal agency in such a manner as to prevent the grazing permittee access to his water.

(c) Prevent agency harassment of private grazing permittees.

(1) Maintenance of accurate range condition records. It shall be a felony malfeasance of office for any employee of the Department of Agriculture or the Department of the Interior to willfully falsify range condition records in such a manner as to depict the private grazing permittee in a false light as a poor or incompetent grazer. Violators shall be subject to a fine of $10,000 and 10 years imprisonment or both.

(2) Entrapment. It shall be a felony malfeasance of office for any employee of the Department of Agriculture or the Department of the Interior to willfully damage fences or to relocate privately owned livestock in such a manner as to make it appear falsely that trespass has occurred. Violators shall be subject to a fine of $10,000 and 10 years imprisonment or both.

Sec. 5. If this Act is found to be in conflict with any previously enacted statute, such conflicting portion of that previously enacted statute shall be considered to be repealed by the relevant portion of this Act and this enactment shall take full precedence for all purposes administrative and judicial.

The Conference regards this model bill as an adequate paradigm for other systems in the overall National Commodity Use System. Other commodity users of the federal lands are encouraged to construct appropriate legislation without delay and to submit it to Congress before commodity uses are completely eliminated on the federal lands.

Wayne Hage, Chairman

National Association of Mining Districts
Tustin, California

Dear President Bush:

The National Association of Mining Districts (NAMD) is an association of Mining Districts in the Western U. S. specifically sanctioned under the federal enabling statute Title 30 of the U.S. Code, section 28. Mineral exploration, identification, inventorying and development on a continuing basis is essential to the maintenance of the strong position of the U.S. as a world economic and military power.

The NAMD is happy to submit the following brief list of items which are significant and essential to the United States:

1. The U.S. Mining Laws relative to the exploration and development of minerals must be preserved.

2. Keeping the vast and public land areas of the Western U.S. open to multiple-use by the public, including open to prospecting and appraising of mineral and energy resources.

3. Preservation of the self-initiation system of mineral exploration and mining claim locations under the U. S. Mining Laws, with consideration of the balance of reasonable filing procedures, reclamation and wilderness areas.

4. Recognition by government agencies of U.S.G.S. Class 4 and 5 roads as routes of travel, as per the U.S. Geological Survey for over 100 years.

5. An organized plan for the identification and inventorying of mineral and energy resources on public lands, with the cooperation of the U.S. Bureau of Mining and other government agencies.

The NAMD will be happy to provide additional data and information on the above, and on the U.S. Mining Laws.

Donald Fife, Chairman
Historical and Cultural Resources Board

Wind River Multiple Use Advocates
Riverton, Wyoming

Dear President Bush,
Over the past twenty years, federal land management agencies have been increasingly experimenting with a philosophy which holds that "nature" is best off where and when human involvement is the least. Many current policies reflect this philosophy, calling for human activities to be held to a minimum. The disastrous spread of Wilderness designations has seriously affected the economies of our Western states.

CONCERNING THE 1988 YELLOWSTONE AREA FIRE SEASON

As uncontrolled wildfires in the Yellowstone area have engulfed an area one third again larger than the state of Rhode Island, the Wind River Multiple Use Advocates call for a vigorous investigation of the policies and management philosophies that allowed the wildfires to get out of control.

At the time this call is being issued, the wildfires have raged over more than one million acres. They have affected more than 1,562 square miles. Before they were finally contained, the wildfires devastated an area as large as the state of Delaware (2,057 square miles).

Without becoming involved in the discussion over whether national park and forest service officials made wise decisions this fire season under existing policies and management philosophies, WRMUA charges that the rampaging wildfires prove that the existing policies and philosophies are unwise.

Over the past 20 years, federal land management agencies have been increasingly experimenting with a philosophy that holds that "nature" is best off where and when human involvement is the least. Many current policies reflect this philosophy, calling for human activities to be held to a minimum.

Simple questions arise: If this nature-without-humans philosophy is really valid for this day and age, why will we probably spend in excess of $100 million to battle the wildfires and reclaim damaged areas? If this philosophy is really valid, why not just let these "natural" wildfires burn until "nature" puts them out?

The Yellowstone area fires, WRMUA holds, show the disastrous results that can come from this experimentation and resulting policies.

The current nature-without-humans policies prevented the timely and full use of effective mechanized fire-fighting techniques to keep the early stages of the wildfires under control.

These policies prevented, in the name of protecting relatively small areas from temporary signs of human activities, early use of bulldozers to build fire lines and the air-dropping of fire retardants. While the managers succeeded in preventing such minor marring of several hundred acres, a million of acres of forest and range were ravaged and marred by the uncontrolled wildfires.

These nature-without-humans policies are further flawed in that they did not allow adequate consideration of two known facts:

a. that 91 percent of the forests in the Yellowstone area were "old-aged" forests, which are particularly prone to extensive wildfires, and

b. that the Yellowstone area has been experiencing a period in the weather cycle that is dryer than any experienced for a long time; dry weather conditions make the forests prone to extensive wildfires.

WRMUA holds that until the basic philosophies and policies are changed, the probability will remain high that the remaining forests in the area, if not throughout major portions of the Western United States, will be prone to extensive wildfires. It is time to admit that the nature-without-man experiment has serious flaws, and that we now must turn our attention to finding management solutions in which humans are cast in a more active role.

A major, vigorous investigation of this summer's extensive wildfires is especially needed because federal land managers, and those who support their current policies, have not told the general public about the full effects of the wildfires. They, for the most part, have concentrated on the possible beneficial effects coming from the fires. But they have avoided talking about the possible negative effects.

Some of these probable negative effects are as follows:

1. Catastrophic wildfires. Within the overall area covered by the uncontrolled wildfires, undoubtedly some parts have been scorched by catastrophic wildfires. This means that the wildfire got so intensely hot in localized areas that most of the organic matter, including seed sources, has been consumed by the flames. New growths of trees are

slow to return to such areas. And such areas are subject to excessive soil erosion. Observers of the forests in the Yellowstone area know that some previous catastrophic wildfire areas have not successfully regrown in periods exceeding 25 or 30 years.

2. Wildlife. The number of creatures, from big game to small non-game animals to microorganisms that have been directly killed by the wildfires will probably always remain unknown. Generally, it can be assumed that the bigger the animal, the less likely it would have been burned to death, but that some have died in the flames.

However, beyond the question of whether or not the creatures of the forest have been burned to death, is the bleak reality facing the survivors. Late summer and fall are important times in the life of wild creatures. During this time of the year, they prepare to face the cold and food shortages of winter. the disruption of their normal feeding patterns, the loss of their normal feeding grounds, and the stress of fleeing the raging wildfires will leave many of these surviving animals in poor shape to face the winter. The resulting winter kill of wildlife indirectly caused by wildfire could greatly exceed the deaths resulting directly from the uncontrolled flames.

Fish are also likely to suffer as the streams and lakes are polluted with the ash washing into these bodies of water. Siltation will also increase from increased erosion, especially from areas laid bare by catastrophic wildfires.

For the grizzly bears, many of the concentrations of white bark pine in the Yellowstone area have been in the path of the wildfires. White bark pine nuts are considered to be an important fall source of protein to assist the grizzly to survive the winter.

While it is true that fresh new plant growth

in many of the burnt-over areas will improve the amount of food available to wildlife after this winter and into the next several decades, this advantage will be lost as the new growth matures unless current management policies are changed.

3. Return of nutrients to the soil. the remaining ash, in spite of claims being made by some, will not be a rich source of nutrients for new plant growth (do you cook your food until it is reduced to ashes so it will be more nutritious?). Most of the plant nutrients go up in flame, rather than remaining in the ash. The fire-seared logs that do remain will deteriorate slower than non-seared wood, delaying the return to the soil what nutrients haven't gone up in flame.

4. Visual quality. As mentioned above, in areas of catastrophic wildfires, the forest will be extremely slow in returning. Some of these areas may not grow the beginnings of a good tree cover in our lifetime. But even in those areas where the fire was not catastrophic, the dominant feature of the landscape for several decades will be the standing skeletons of fire-killed trees. These ghastly skeletons will remain to tower over the green growth of new trees on the forest floor.

As the wildfires have raged across the Yellowstone area, officials and their apologists have been releasing statement after statement concerning the benefits that the fires will bring to the area. In many cases, these statements are in direct contradiction to what the same people have been saying over the past several years about the supposed negative effects of commodity uses of the forest.

Throughout our involvement in the various forest planning processes, we have been told that one of the critical requirements for wildlife is the cover/forage ratio. We have been told that hiding and thermal cover is essential -- that in some cases up to 75 percent of an area needs to remain in cover.

We have been told that cover is necessary along routes of wildlife movement from one location to another. Now we are being told that wildfires are good for wildlife, regardless of what the wildfires do to the cover/forage ratio.

We have been told that timber harvesting of relatively small areas of the forest changes the migration patterns of big game, especially elk. Now we are told that wildfires clearing thousands upon thousands of acres of forest will not affect wildlife migration patterns.

We have been told that disturbances of relatively few acres of land by commodity uses will lead to excessive erosion and land slides. Yet these problems haven't been associated with wildfires laying bare thousands upon thousands of acres of the forest.

We have been told that commodity uses of the forest will ruin the visual quality of the forest landscape. Now we are told that the thousands upon thousands of acres ravished by wildfires will be beautiful green meadows by next spring.

We have been told that commodity uses will make the forests unsuited for recreational uses. the future effect of the wildfire-scarred forests on recreational uses seems to have been ignored.

We have been told that the air pollution in Los Angeles is a threat to human health. Now we are told that we shouldn't worry about the smoke pollution extending hundreds of miles from the wildfires, because the resulting air quality is no worse than that of Los Angeles.

It seems impossible to us that a relatively minor disturbance of the forest, because it is human induced, would be fatal to the forest in one instance -- but a vastly greater disturbance, because it is "natural," completely lacks any negative consequences in another instance.

In summary, WRMUA holds that the lack of

candid information requires that a vigorous investigation be conducted in order that the American public can fully appreciate the full impacts -- both positive and negative -- of the extensive wildfires in the Yellowstone area during the 1988 fire season.

Further, we believe that the wildfires have resulted from the application of flawed policies and management philosophies. The investigation should center on the need to change these policies and philosophies.

We support the people of the Wise Use Movement as a living example of mankind for nature, nature for mankind.

George Reynolds
President

National Park Users Association
Bellevue, Washington

Dear President Bush,

The National Park Users Association is a nationwide citizen organization that acts to save public access to our national park system. We grew because organizations calling themselves "environmentalists" have succeeded in closing off public access to our precious national parks through the destruction of concessions and establishment of rationing programs to limit the number of visitors to the national parks.

Congress in 1916 gave the National Park Service the double mandate of preserving park features unimpaired for future generations and of managing the parks for public use and enjoyment. Our experience has shown that the National Park Service has violated its congressional mandate and needs strict oversight from both the Secretary of the Interior and the Congress. The National Park

Service has become a separate kingdom within the government that acts according to its own preferences and responds only to the wishes of environmentalist organizations in changing policy.

Saving the National Parks for Public Use
      THE NATIONAL PARKS REFORM ACT: To create protective agencies for our natural heritage of a size conducive to responsible management and accessible to congressional oversight. Creates within the Department of the Interior, under authority of the Assistant Secretary for Fish and Wildlife and Parks four separate agencies each with its own director responsible for management of our current oversized and jumbled national park system: Reorganizes the National Park Service, with new management responsibility limited to only those units officially designated "national parks" and "national monuments" in the "natural" category; creates the National Urban Park Service with management responsibility for all units of the park system in urban settings designed primarily for contemplation, enlightenment or inspiration such as the National Capitol Parks; creates the National Recreational Park Service with management responsibility for all National Recreation Areas of the park system and other units primarily used for recreational purposes; creates the National Historical Park Service with management responsibility for all national historic parks and similar units of primarily historic interest.
      The present National Park Service with its domain in excess of 80 million acres has grown into a bureaucracy so huge and powerful that it can ignore the public will, the intent of Congress and direct orders of the Secretary of the Interior with impunity. Such concentrated power cannot be allowed to persist within a representative form of government. This Act will separate out from the

present conglomeration of diverse units four different kinds of national heritage lands that have previously been lumped together into a single vast and unresponsive agency. The new arrangement will group together those that are naturally similar for appropriate management to protect the essential character of each different kind of park.

STRICT OVERSIGHT: Environmentalists have recommended that the National Park Service be removed from the Department of the Interior and set up as a separate agency "to remove it from political influences." Such a move would in fact place the Park Service in the exact center of political influences where powerful environmentalist groups could manipulate its policy with certain control, eliminating visitors and shutting down visitor concessions. Instead, these measures must be taken in order to preserve the parks for the people:

1. The respective committees of the House of Representatives and the Senate should form a special subcommittee of National Park Oversight with investigative and prosecutorial powers to insure that the agency follows congressional intent in its administration of park laws.

2. The Secretary of the Interior and the Assistant Secretary of fish and Wildlife and Parks should be given increased powers to demand accountability, and to check and veto the actions of the Director of the National Park Service and lower executives of the agency.

MISSION 2010: ADEQUATE VISITOR ACCOMMODATIONS: The Concession Policy Act of 1965 should be extended to all facilities of the NPS. A major thrust should be made to properly accommodate the increased visitor load on our parks through a 20-year construction program of new concessions including overnight accommodations, restoration and reconstruction of classic rustic lodges, campgrounds and visitor service stores in all 48

national parks, with priority given to Great Smoky
Mountain, Everglades, Rocky Mountain, Big Bend,
Canyonlands, Sequoia, Redwoods, North Cascades,
Denali, and Theodore Roosevelt. Concession restoration should begin immediately in Yellowstone
(West Thumb). The lodge at Manzanita Lake in
Lassen Volcanic National Park, which was demolished by the National Park Service, shall be rebuilt
in replica on its original site and become the first
project of Mission 2010, to become known as the Don
Hummel Memorial Lodge honoring the late outstanding leader of the national park concession
movement.

Appropriate overnight visitor facilities should
be constructed in all national monuments, national
recreation areas, and major historical areas. Policies that exclude people shall be outlawed by congress. The possessory interest of the private concessioner should be maximized. Private firms with
expertise in people-moving such as Walt Disney
should be selected as transportation concessioners
to accommodate and enhance the national park
experience for all visitors.

All actions designed to exclude park visitors
such as shutting down overnight accommodations
and rationing entry should be eliminated as inimical to the mandate of Congress for "public use and
enjoyment" in the National Park Act of 1916. Severe criminal penalties of felony malfeasance of
office shall be levied against offending agency
employees who recommend or put in action any plan
to limit public access to the national parks, with
fines up to $10,000 and prison terms up to ten years.

What can we do to stop the national parks
from being stolen from the public? First, keep in
mind the truth about the big lies:

1) The Truth: The natural integrity of our
National Parks is not threatened by visitors. Even
the four or five most-used parks suffer crowding

very few days of the year. The carrying capacity of the entire park system is immense and barely touched. Visitor loads should be accommodated by developing additional overnight facilities at dispersed sites with the national parks, not shut out altogether by the destruction of concession facilities. As respected scientist J. E. Lovelock pointed out in his widely acclaimed book *Gaia: A New Look at Life on Earth*, nature is not as fragile as the environmentalists would have you believe. President Bush, protect our rights of access!

2) The Truth: Wilderness is not an evocative general term, it is an official government designation that keeps the vast majority of the world's citizens from visiting more than 80 million acres of America. Official Wilderness means absolutely no development. Make national parks available for people's use and enjoyment. Gradually phase out wilderness designations within national parks.

3) The Truth: Environmentalism has more on the agenda than protecting nature, it has distinctly anti-people overtones that are hidden and denied but that nevertheless powerfully impact our national policy. Environmentalists may tell you anything. Be skeptical.

4) The Truth: The media refuse to tell the visitors' and concessioners' side of the national park story and make a mere pretense of objectivity by devoting a few quotes to concessioners while carefully explaining environmentalist views. Be skeptical.

5) The Truth: The Park Service is a working partner in stealing the national parks despite its claims of innocence and its haughty dismissal of critics. They work in obscurity, bow politely to the Mather-Albright principles of visitor accommodation, and do what they please. Don't trust them.

But just keeping your eye on the truth isn't enough. A practical, down-to-earth activist program is the basis of all change in this country. If we want to preserve public use and enjoyment of our national parks, then we have to fight for it. The opposition is powerful and intelligent, but they can be beaten.

Here's a blueprint for success:
Future Needs:

Exposing Anti-Concession, Anti-Access Intent

All National Park policies should be analyzed by Congress for anti-concession, anti-access intent and consequence. This analysis should become a required part of every Master Plan, Environmental Assessment, and Environmental Impact Statement. The relevant laws must be amended to reflect such anti-concession, anti-access intent reporting requirement. The true anti-private enterprise intent of environmentalists too often is hidden in deceptive words and seductive phrases. A "hard-look" doctrine needs to be brought to every step of the National Park planning process to explicitly state whether any given policy will harm or help concessions and public access. The findings must be stated in clear, plain English. Public criminal and private civil penalties should be imposed against any Park Service employee or pressure group representative who attempts to hide or disguise the harmful effect of a policy on concessions and public access. A private attorney general provision must be enacted to provide payment of attorney fees, court costs and damage awards to members of the public who bring lawsuits against the agency or environmental groups. Park-access organizations should have the right to sue the Park Service and environmental groups on behalf of the general public for denying public access to the national parks.

Release of Information on Anti-Concession, Anti-Access Lobbying Groups

A Right-To-Know measure concerning environmental groups should be adopted. It should require any group that lobbies or otherwise pressures agencies or legislatures to adopt policies with the intent or consequence of limiting national park public access to disclose the names and addresses of its sources of income including private memberships, donations, and grants. The salaries of all officers should likewise be released. The public is entitled to know who wants to keep it out of its own national parks and how much they're paying their lobbyists to keep you out.

Sell-Backs: Uniting Ownership With Operation

Strengthening concession ability to manage is essential to ending the bureaucratic mess imposed on public services in the parks at the demand of environmentalists. One of the most sensible programs would be to sell back to private parties all government-owned public service facilities in the parks. Another would be to place new private facilities in park areas where public demand exists. Still another is to increase the concessioner's investment so as to increase his incentive to manage well in order to make a profit. All possessory interests that have been seized from concessioners by agency contract abrogation should be *given* back to the concessioner or his successor along with a penalty payment of ten times the value of the concession for denial of private enterprise.

Increasing Protections

The present degraded state of concession policy is a direct result of environmentalist pressure on a few congressmen who were willing to wreck the Concession Policy Act of 1965 for the sake of political popularity. The power of all congressional committees other than the House Interior and Insular Affairs Committee and the Senate Energy and Environment Committee to create national park policy should be statutorily limited and ultimately eliminated. As opportunities arise, steps toward refocusing national park oversight into its proper committee should be taken.

Enlightening Park Service Oversight

Park Service control over virtually every aspect of a concessioner's operation and public access is complete. Unfortunately, Service personnel entertain strongly anti-private-enterprise attitudes and are vastly ignorant and incompetent to run business operations. Civil Service guidelines for all concession specialists should require degrees in business administration and previous experience in a successful for-profit, non-government private enterprise. Universities should offer degree programs for the national park concession specialist stressing the needs of profit-making private enterprise in a public land setting.

Interior Department Reorganization

Wallace Stegner once said the national parks are one of the best ideas we ever had. We agree. Unfortunately, the National Park Service cannot be ranked in that high category. A new Interior Department Division of Mandate Protection is obviously needed to keep the balance between use vs. preservation closer to center. This division should be situated in the present Solicitor's Office with a corresponding legal overseer from the Secretary of the Interior's office assigned within the National Park Service with powers to open any file and challenge any action. All Park Service files should be open to the Division of Mandate Protection. This division should have the legal authority to nullify any Park Service policy that strays too far from a genuine balance between use and prservation. The solicitor is the only Interior Department officer with the legal power to stop even the Secretary dead in his tracks and is less susceptible to the pressuring of environmentalist groups. Without such a reorganization, public access to our precious parks is doomed to slow strangulation.

The Need for Continual Reassessment

Growing pressure on park access by self-serving environmental groups, coupled with increasing demands for visitor access, create a continual need to reassess the place of environmentalist dogma in national park management. Changes will not come rapidly. Park Service policy is already clear in dealing with environmentalist pressure: bow down and ignore public access. The Park Service must be made to understand its legal responsibility to provide "public use and enjoyment" of the parks for the common person and not just for the highly sensitive and elite nature lover. The non-affiliated park-going public must be included in the policy decision-making process to bring some balance to the present overwhelming domination by large powerful environmental organizations that are out to exclude the general unaffiliated public.

The Personal Touch

What can just one person do? A lot! Many public issues have been won by the concerned action of a single person. Here's a list of a dozen actions from the easy to the hard to accomplish.

1. If you're a member of an environmental group (and about five million of us are) and you didn't realize your organization was doing such things as I've revealed in this book, you can do several things:

A: Ask your group leaders what their policy is about national park concessions. Ask them what they think of access for everyone to the national parks. Ask them what they think about overnight accommodations in the parks.

B: Insist that a Parks Are For People policy be adopted by your environmental group's local chapter and the national organization. If they don't

want to talk about it, make it an issue.
It's your group.

C. Get your environmental organization to put together a periodic
Concession Appreciation Day. Take
people to the parks to enjoy the natural beauty and include a meeting with
a concession representative. They'll
be happy to tell you what their concession does and show you around.

2. If you're a member of a social or civic group,
have a meeting on the national park situation.
Have a speaker, a discussion, a debate. Get the
issues out in the open.

3. Start a local Concession History Society
centered around your nearest national park concession. You'd be surprised how little historical knowledge has actually been collected and preserved by
concessioners -- they've been slightly busy housing
and feeding a few hundred million people, minding
the store, and coping with a few floods and snow-
storms here and there. There's a wealth of material
just waiting for an interested organizer and inter-
preter.

Concession history is an area where volunteer citizen help can make a truly meaningful differ-
ence. The more we know about a subject the more
we appreciate its significance. There are many
national park history societies, but not many national park concession history societies. Old papers
by the thousands are just stuffed away in back
rooms here and there waiting for interested people
to bring the past alive. Tape record interviews with
retired concessioners. Make your trips to the national parks a personal experience by finding out
about the people who accommodated the people.

4. Take on national park concessions as your
personal cause. If you're looking for something to
do, there's a lot to be done. People must be informed.

The threat of losing our precious access to the national parks must be explained. The role of concessions in keeping the parks open must be made clear to everyone. As you can see by this book, concessioning is an involved subject. It needs good interpreters among those who have never been concessioners. It needs good people to explain it to others. It needs citizen champions to stand up for it in the public limelight.

5. Buy a share of concessioner stock. It won't cost much and it won't earn much, but it will be a symbol of your support for open parks and sound park concessions.

6. Join the National Park Users Association. A number of national groups touch on concession issues. It's an action-oriented public interest group that doesn't mind fighting for your right to use our precious national parks.

7. Get political. Support candidates of any party who pledge to support public use and enjoyment of the national parks and respect for the Mather-Albright principles of sound national park concessions. Let your own congressman and those who serve on the House Interior and Insular Affairs Committee and the Senate Energy and Environment Committee know how you feel about access to your national parks.

8. Be informed about Park Service actions. Receive their notices of intent to close down accommodations, campgrounds, and trails -- you can get your name added to the Park Service mailing list by writing to Director, National Park Service, Washington, D.C., 20240. Attend NPS public meetings to let your voice be heard. If you can't attend, write your comments and urge your friends to do the same.

9. Let the National Park Service know directly what you think about public access to public lands. Remind them that you're the landlord and they're just the hired help. Put the same kind of pressure on them to keep the parks open for people -- all kinds of people -- that the environmental groups put on them to keep people out. If we complain loud enough long enough they'll bend to our pressure instead.

Eugenia Hummel
Board of Directors

Timber Association of California
Sacramento, California

Dear President Bush,
The United States is a net importer of wood products. Last year, we imported 12.2 billion board feet more softwood lumber than we exported. In wholesale lumber terms, that volume represents between $2 billion and $2.5 billion -- dollars that are contributing to an unfavorable trade balance. It is also nearly one-fourth of our total softwood consumption.
The harvesting of federally-owned timber (Forest Service, BLM, and others) generates more than one billion dollars annually in taxes of all kinds, and the private timber harvest adds another two billion. The imported lumber represents foregone taxes in an amount nearly equivalent to that generated by federal timber harvest.
The forest lands of this nation have the productive capacity to turn us from net importers to net exporters of solid wood products.

William Denison
President

Consumer Alert
Modesto, California

Dear President Bush,

Consumer Alert is a nationwide consumer advocacy group with members in all fifty states. CA is funded by voluntary dues contributed by its members, by foundation grants and by sale of publications.

ON WISE LAND-USE POLICY

The environmental movement, although initially begun to make Americans more aware of the need to solve various ecological problems resulting from years of inattention to environmental affairs, today has taken on a life of its own involved only with maintaining its status as a going concern.

Movement leaders, more and more often referred to as anti-growth advocates, coercive utopians, and even fear mongers, show telltale signs of fanaticism. There is no rational basis to their negative pronouncements on mining of precious minerals, well managed forestry or prudent petroleum development.

American consumers are harmed when restrictions are placed on the wise development of natural resources. Consumers benefit from the efficient and ecologically sound development of all resources found in nature.

Housing costs rise when our national timber industry is saddled with unreasonable restrictions and is precluded from harvesting timber at a cost lower than imported supply. Likewise, higher costs of all timber-related products such as paper and packaging result when domestic harvesting is rendered uncompetitive by unreasonable federal regulations.

On behalf of American consumers, we urge that the federal government reconsider present restrictive forest policy and preservationists artificial scarcity and move toward wise use and development of our nation's natural resources. We urge that a careful and reasonable balance be struck between consumer needs and demands and available supply of our nation's natural resources.

ON HARVESTING TIMBER

Recognizing that societal concerns will include the aesthetic provision of wooded lands within urban communities, and granting that it is a legitimate role of government to determine how much forest land shall be set aside and withheld from lumbering for environmental and recreational purposes, the guaranteed rights that are inherent in private ownership must nevertheless be safeguarded.

There can be no justification for imposing "sustained yield" (i.e. if you harvest a tree, you must plant a tree), upon private landowners in a free society.

Timber is a renewable resource. the private timber owner has every reason to look to his own long-term interest in renewing his forest.

Basic economics dictate that society's continuing demand for lumber for homebuilding, furniture and paper products will be met one way or another. If America's lumber industry is prevented by a myriad of inflexible and ill-conceived regulations from filling that demand, imports of timber from countries with less stringent regulations will fill that demand. Increases in imported timber, aside from the economic impact, should be of concern to those who profess a genuine concern for forest preservation throughout the world because many nations are lacking in any forest planning whatsoever, and even greater forest depletion may occur as a result.

Other than the fact that it takes several years

for trees to regrow after harvest, the timber industry is not unlike any other industry. Trees, unlike commodities such as petroleum, are a renewable natural resource.

Each time government imposes limits on the amount that can be harvested (often in response to a vocal minority committed to "saving the trees"), several unforeseen things happen. First, the price of goods made from timber rises because of the reduced supply, or even the anticipated reduced supply. Housing, paper goods, furniture and other timber related consumer products become more expensive. Second, as lumber commands a higher market price, incentives increase for new entrants into the timber industry and those in the industry are encouraged to harvest even more while the price is up. third, politicization of the timber market makes even the most prudent manager unsure and more likely to forego long-range planning for an early harvest with less restocking investment.

The only way to ensure that national forest land, both public and private, continues to yield sufficient supplies to satisfy consumer demand while keeping pace with adequate investment in regeneration is to let market forces work, free of unpredictable and irrational political pressure. This will only be possible when decision-makers take the time to observe and make the effort to understand the predictable results of competitive enterprise.

One could easily make the same claims about beef cattle that one often hears with regard to timber: "If we harvest cows for food and other consumer products, the earth will sooner or later be devoid of cows." In fact, just the opposite has happened, in a market that determines its own rate of harvest and re-generation, and where consumer demand determines the price, cows have dramatically increased in number, for it is economically beneficial to the rancher to restock his herd and look

to the future.
     In a free market, trees will surely follow the same path.
     In particular, Consumer Alert stands in solidarity with the people of the Wise Use Movement in their struggle to supply the world's consumers with products and the American economy with jobs.

Barbara Keating
Executive Director

International Association of Snowmobile Administrators

Dear President Bush,
     Americans today spend more time and more dollars on recreation than ever before. At the same time, the number of different recreational activities has soared. This increase in recreation is very evident on America's trails, but in most cases, this expanded demand has not been matched by expanded supply. The result has been a growing problem in providing quality trail experiences.
     In some cases, however, trail systems have been expanded to meet demand in states where legislation has been passed requiring registration of snowmobiles, motorcycles and ATV's, and the earmarking of a portion of the registration receipts for a state trails program for these activities. State taxes on fuel used in these vehicles have also been made available to trail programs in some states. The President's Commission on Americans Outdoors recognized the effectiveness of these programs and recommended that federal fuel tax receipts generated by motorized vehicles used off-highway be used to aid recreation, much as federal motorboat fuel taxes are through the Wallop-Breaux Trust Fund.

Trail enthusiasts using motorized vehicles pay at least $83.5 million in federal gasoline taxes annually which are used to construct highways, not to aid motorized recreation programs. These monies should instead be returned to a National Recreation Trails Trust Fund. The fund would provide matching grants to state and federal agencies, local governments and private trail groups, coordinated through appropriate state agencies, with the primary goal of encouraging multiple-use trail development. A provision should also be made for adding additional revenues to the fund in the future, revenues derived from trail activities that do not generate fuel taxes.

NATIONAL RECREATION TRAILS TRUST FUND PROPOSAL

Legislation establishing the National Recreation Trails Trust Fund should incorporate the following points:

● The U.S. Department of the Interior should administer the program using no more than 5% of annual receipts for dispersing funds and providing technical assistance.

● The Department of the Treasury should determine the amount of federal taxes paid on fuel used in motorized recreation vehicles used off-road within five years after enactment, and periodically thereafter.

● Grants should be made available primarily for trail development, but maintenance, easement acquisition, and facility development would be eligible as well.

● State eligibility for grants would be automatic for four years, and thereafter dependent upon:

(1)   State action to set aside fuel

taxes paid by motorized off-road recreationists (or equivalent general fund revenues); and

       (2)   establishment of a state trail advisory board.

    ●   Partnerships with private landowners would be encouraged.

    ●   A national trails advisory board, representing trail users, and including federal officials as ex officio members, would be established.

    ●   Two-thirds of the total grant monies would be reserved for projects open to at least some motorized trail enthusiasts.

    ●   A maximum of 5% of the monies would be available for environmental and safety information programs.

    ●   50% of the available grant monies would be divided equally among eligible states.

    ●   50% of monies would be divided among eligible states based on the number of vehicles used off-road in each state.

    ●   A maximum of 60% of a project's cost would be paid with federal funds for multiple-use trails that include motorized use; a 40% federal match would be available for limited-use trails.

    ●   A 25% federal cost share would be allowed for facilities development and maintenance, although maintenance projects would further require 25% cash or "in-kind" match from trail enthusiasts.

    ●   Monies not expended by a state within two years would be reclaimed and would be available for redistribution by the Secretary of the Interior through a national, merit-based competition.

    The National Recreation Trails Trust Fund is not intended to replace or compete with ongoing funding mechanisms like the Land and Water Conservation Fund. Rather, it is designed to provide an equitable return of monies to the states to fund specific programs that benefit trail enthusiasts.

Roy Muth

(Mr. Muth's statement is similar to but not identical with Mr. Clark Collins' statement for the Blue Ribbon Coalition above. The statements were derived through cooperation of related groups that agree on many points but may vary in their stands upon specific items.)

National Association of Reversionary Property Owners
Issaquah, Washington

Dear President Bush,

PROPERTY RIGHTS PROTECTION
    Railroad easements when abandoned by the original or successor operating railroad company shall revert to the underlying adjacent or abutting property owner according to pertinent state law. No easement on an abandoned or non-used railroad right-of-way shall be given by government decree to a "Rails To Trails" program without payment of just compensation plus money damages for loss of economic opportunity to the adjacent or abutting property owner who holds the reversionary interest to the land.

AVOIDANCE OF UNANTICIPATED "TAKINGS" BY THE FEDERAL GOVERNMENT
    In March 1988, Executive Order 12630 was issued by the President. Independent federal regulatory agencies as defined in 44 USC 3502(10) were specifically eliminated from the Executive Order. There are certain independent regulatory agencies

that are on the list in 44 USC 3502(10) that, in their regular course of agency action, get into the possible realm of "taking" private property. Legislation should be passed by Congress that would allow these certain independent regulatory agencies to be included in Executive Order 12630.

Richard Welsh
Executive Director

James D. Petersen
Grants Pass, Oregon

Dear President Bush,
        Here are recommendations I wish to make for the Wise Use Agenda:
        1. A minimum management requirement for timber production on all publicly owned forestlands. We have MMR's for spotted owls and most game animals. why not timber? Isn't the productivity of the nation's timberlands as important to the environment as protection for wildlife?
        2. Legislation preventing the National Park Service from ever again being able to take over national forest lands. The tragic lesson of Yellowstone speaks to the incompetence of the Park Service in a way words cannot.
        3. Legislation that provides adequate fire protection for the nation's forests. Translation: ROADS IN ALL REMAINING UNROADED AREAS. We're losing these areas to wildfire at a rate that far exceeds the most ambitious harvesting scheme.

James D. Petersen
Advertising and public relations consultant to the forest industry

Washington County Commission
St. George, Utah

Dear President Bush,

Washington County, Utah recommends clear policy guidance to federal agencies that will clarify and define the rights of local governments to claim public rights of way under the provisions of Revised Statute 2477 (formerly codified at 43 CFR 932). This statute allows local governments to use, maintain and improve public roads that cross federal lands and that existed prior to October 21, 1976.

WILDERNESS POLICY

Washington County, Utah recommends that all future wilderness designations exclude areas containing resources necessary to the economic well-being of the affected local residents. Also, the management of designated wilderness areas must provide for the necessary public access to maintain resources including but not limited to water, minerals, timber, rangeland and intensive recreation uses.

SUSTAINED MULTIPLE USE PRINCIPLES

Washington County, Utah is highly dependent upon federal lands, which comprise 75.8 percent of the county land base. It is essential that these federal lands be managed so as to allow appropriate multiple uses. Attempts by narrow interest groups and federal agencies to restrict land uses on federal lands should be reviewed and closely coordinated with affected local governments.

Jerry B. Lewis
Chairman

Seneca Sawmill Company
Eugene, Oregon

Dear President Bush,

The Forest Service has several million dollars for public relations, such as in the Smokey the Bear and Lassie campaigns. They have done a very creditable job in getting the public aware of fires and the damage to lands and all of the creatures that live there. In turn, they have done very little in telling about commodity uses of the forests, the benefits both economically and in improving the forests for new trees, winter grazing in the newly harvested areas, and so forth. They never show that trees do grow back with the water quality still protected. They have failed to show all of the special work that is being done to enhance the streams for fish. In most cases, the information is presented in dull fashion. I want the Forest Service committed to put as much information about commodities as they do about Wilderness. I want the story told in a fascinating way, so that people will read and understand the other side of the wise use of the forests.

Therefore, I suggest the following to be a part of the message to the new administration:

"The Secretaries of Agriculture and Interior shall utilize the talents of their public affairs departments to publicize and explain all of the social and economic benefits of the multiple use of the forest and their interrelationship."

Arnold Ewing

United Four Wheel Drive Associations of U.S. and Canada
Felton, Pennsylvania

Dear President Bush,

Our organization has long been deeply involved in working to keep our public lands open to all of the public, not just for certain selfish elites.

The current state of recreation on public lands in this country is rapidly approaching a crisis. This crisis is that the vast majority of public land users are being locked off of more and more of their National and State Forests and BLM lands. This loss of access is steadily increasing even though these user groups are deeply involved in cooperative projects like Adopt-a-Trail/Road and strong demand is registered for motorized and other multiple use activities. National Forest user surveys show typically only 2-5% of Forest use on Wilderness and similar singular use areas. Yet most Forests have much more than this percentage locked off in Wilderness or similar categories, some as much as 50%. Yet the incessant demands for more continue as shown by efforts like the Cranston Wilderness Bill.

Another problem that contributes heavily to this crisis is that these demands have received disproportionate favor with public land officials and planners. In one National Forest plan, input requesting more 4WD opportunities was approximately a third of all input, yet the planners failed to recognize any significant demand for or plan for any 4WD use. Also available to these planners was a state outdooor recreation study that documented that 4WD recreation ranked 11th in total activity, compared to 13th for hiking and 19th for hunting. In comparison, the facilities (supply/demand%) available statewide to meet the recreational demand ranked at 87% for hiking and 112% for hunting, yet only 9% for 4WD recreation and 4% for ORV/ ATV recreation. Even with this data and a strong demonstration of demand, the planners recommended a blanket closure of the forest to 4WD and ORV trail use.

We strongly request that the recreation resources match the actual demand and reverse the present imbalance.

There is a pressing need for a realistic definition of "roadless" when it comes to definition of land and designation for wilderness and "roadless." We have seen areas with improved gravel roads designated wilderness by bureaucratic fiat by merely gating the road in question, then imagining it no longer exists. The classification of "roadless areas" must be made consistent with FS policy of classing any primitive travelway (over 40-50 inches wide) as a road, and not disregarding them out of convenience just because they are closed.

We request that "roadless" areas be re-evaluated solely on whether any roads primitive or otherwise exist. If there are any roads inside these areas, they should be re-evaluated for SPM use in adequately dispersing 4WD and ORV use of the forest and policy. Where an area is genuinely roadless, we strongly prefer that the area remain roadless, undeveloped, uncut, and managed to emphasize primitive recreation to offset areas opened to motorized use.

The issue of user conflict is another area of inconsistent and capricious management, which is desperately in need of fundamental revision. It seems that whenever user conflict is even suggested, the road or trail in question is always closed to 4WD or ORV use. It is ludicrous when a previously open and existing jeep road must be closed (because of "user conflict") when someone decides to relocate a hiking trail onto this route. 4WD and ORV recreation have a high potential for "user conflict" and is not an equally acceptable use of the forest. Frequently "user conflict" is not analyzed with other types of recreation. The myth of "user conflict" is primarily a perceived problem used against motorized recreation created by the same selfish minority that is not willing to share the recreational assets of public lands. yet most public land management remain unwilling to recognize this, and to justly resolve these "user conflicts."

We would like to request that you change the management definition of "ORV" to reflect actual and real use of public land. Four wheel drive vehicles, or Recreational Four Wheelers as we prefer, primarily use existing roads, primitive forest roads, and travelways that are referred to as jeep trails on topography maps for access to remote areas of the forest for enjoyment of nature through camping, fishing, hunting, hiking, picknicking, climbing, canoeing, and many other ends designed to "get away from things." An ORV is a trail vehicle designed primarily for cross-country use. Four wheel drive users include many fishermen, campers, many or probably most hunters, and the like. This access has not been opposed heavily in most places and is not a significant part of the generic opposition to ORV use.

Most managers fail to consider management alternatives that adequately disperse the use of ORV and 4WD vehicles evenly over all districts. Many fail to address any solutions to the conflicts between the users and refuse to consider user-cooperative programs that would enable areas to be open with fewer management problems.

We request a thorough revision of public land plans to reflect the needs of the large sector of the public who have proven substantial demand for motorized recreation. Manage the primitive roads/ 4WD travelways open except where posted closed. Establish a substantial open network of 4WD primitive roads which will adequately disperse usage to avoid unacceptable resource damage. Model the management strategy after that developed on forest Service Region 8 ORV policy, which has proven a success.

We strongly request that these plans be revised to reflect the following policies on all public

lands:
    1. Manage the primitive Forest roads open, unless signed closed.
    2. Explicitly define a road as any travelway greater than 40-50 inches in width.
    3. Provide an extensive open system of 4WD roads to disperse use and avoid resource damage from closure-caused overconcentration.
    4. Use cooperative user programs such as Adopt-a-Trail/Road to assist in management solutions.

    In summary, we request that you provide for four wheel drive recreation on the vast existing network of primitive travelways to:
    ●   Address the growing demand for 4WD recreation.
    ● Satisfy increasing need to disperse camping and other uses on the forests.
    ●   Provide for the increasing need of the growing elderly and handicapped sectors of the population for access to the forests.
    ● Utilize the increasing popularity of user-cooperative programs as Adopt-a-Trail/Road to assist in the management.

    We call for an end to placing more and more of the National Forests locked off from a large sector of the public. Some forests now have over half the forest dedicated to wilderness-type use, which usually serves no more than a few percent of the total recreational use. this has occurred through disproportionate concessions to the Wilderness Society/ Sierra Club interests. If the current trend continues, there will be little forest left open to serve the vast majority of users producing much greater resource impacts and levels of user conflicts. We encourage you to assess the cumulative impacts of this trend and rectify this problem by more equitable management policies.

Four wheel drive use of public lands is a growing use in step with the future, which emphasizes dispersed, undeveloped, back-country recreation. A fundamental redirection of public land management toward recreation must recognize that many users require motorized means to reach remote areas of public lands to camp, fish, bird-watch, hunt, hike, and explore in a reasonable time period. The higher mobility of handicapped and the growing elderly sector of the population require motorized means to experience the beauty of nature in remote areas. the vast amount of National Forest and BLM land can serve to disperse some of the load of overcrowded National Parks if properly managed and people are directed toward the rich, undeveloped recreational opportunities. You will find user groups willing to assist if the management will stop closure-dominant policies and be responsive to a balanced section of users instead of pushy minorities.

Special interest arrangementss such as Wilderness serve no useful purpose, but cause substantial problems. We suggest broad accessible recreational-emphasis management categories for public lands that conserve the pristine qualities by limiting development while emphasizing all types of dispersed and undeveloped back-country recreation. Four wheel drive recreation will interface well with this strategy if adequate mileage is open to widely disperse the usage. Please reverse past preference of preservationist interests in favor of a balanced management. We strongly recommend that careful consideration be given to the problems we raise so past inequities may be repaired with fresh, new, and balanced management strategies.

David L. Hook
Director of Environmental Affairs

Intermountain Community Alliance for Resources and Environment (ICARE)
Burney, California

Dear President Bush,

As you are no doubt aware, the impact of the current Spotted Owl Reserve policy on timber harvest is substantial, in terms of the potential harvest volume, which will be lost from the Western National Forests. These dedicated Owl areas will reduce the timber volume available to local mills, and thus has become a very emotional issue to the Intermountain communities of Northern California, as well as of the entire Northwest. We have many timber dependent communities that are in danger of suffering great loss to their economies if this issue is not solved by policy makers other than the Regional Foresters of the U.S. Forest Service. Environmentalists whose actual goal is to destroy our timber economy claim that spotted owls require "old growth" timber as nesting sites. In fact, we see spotted owls nesting in second growth stands every day, but environmentalists and their hired scientists corrupt the truth by ignoring or denying that scientific fact. We believe that you and the Secretary of Agriculture are the individuals who can and must determine whether owls are in fact endangered and whether owls are more important than people.

We see and hear everyday in California, and in the Northwest, that the "radical environmentalists" are winning victories in cases that are deciding which lands will be set aside for "no-use," without consideration of the effect on people. We believe that the spotted owl reserve plan is one such case, and that there is in fact, no concrete evidence that the Owl needs the amount of old growth that the Audubon Society and others claim. In fact, as we mentioned above, the owl has been found nesting in many second growth areas that the Audubon Society claims are entirely unsuitable habitat. In our local area, the Owl has been found nesting in young growth stands and even in cut over areas. But still these "radicals" persist with the claim that Owls need pristine old growth. In this area, Owl territories will cause a reduction of approximately 25 to 30 million board feet of old growth timber per year. The fact is that each one million board feet of timber provides 15 jobs, so we are talking about the possibility of losing 450 jobs in our area alone. I believe, however, that there is a solution to the above problem and would like to make a proposal.

The following proposal was made to the Regional Forester of the Southwest Region, in the Spring of 1988. Locally, the Pit River canyon is already being managed for Bald Eagles and Falcons, and there is one Owl territory also in place. Though the local U.S. Forest Service has been unsuccessful in getting Owls to respond to calling, we have seen Spotted owls in the area described many times. Our proposal to the U.S. Forest Service called for the existing Owl territory to be extended down the river to the Forest boundary, a distance of approximately 6 miles, making the total acreage involved about 6,500. This would give the two National Forests involved an opportunity to abandon Owl territories in other locations that are productive for timber, and would provide an area that really is not suitable for anything but "bird management."

Any future considerations for Owl territories would require that they be placed within Wilderness Areas or Resource Natural Areas, or other areas not considered to be Commercial Timberland. The Regional Forester did not answer our letter, and in fact, is planning the addition of several Owl territories recommended by the Audubon Society. This means that there will be additional acreage taken out of timber production, and with only 25% of the National Forest acres in the 12 Western States available for full Timber Management now, will only serve to compound the problem of future timber supply. This will ensure the failure of many small businesses, which are dependent on our National Forests for their business, and future. We believe that the use of the Spotted Owl, which by the way is not on the Endangered list, or the use of any other creature of the woods, which the "radicals" choose to name as a surrogate to their cause, and which by affording additional protection, infringes on the livelihood of mankind, should be against the law, and should be a punishable crime.

It is apparent that the battle is not over with regard to which species should receive protection, and which ones should not. However, the fact remains that over 75% of our National Forests in the Western States are already in some scheme of "set aside," either as Designated Wilderness, Designated Roadless, Scenic and Wild rivers, Resource Natural Areas, old Growth Retention, Scenic Road Corridors, Wildlife Preserves, and many other constrained areas, too numerous to mention here.

The cry of the communities in the Intermountain area, and in the Northwest is that we cannot survive with the Owl management scheme that is being implemented in Western States National Forests today. You must understand that we are fighting for our lives. Families will be uprooted, and lives will be destroyed. Businesses will fail, and the economy of the Intermountain area will crumble. The school districts will suffer losses because of reduced 25% funds, and school programs will be eliminated. As families move from the area, school enrollment will decrease, meaning a reduction of state monies, as well as reductions in teaching staffs.

All of this is the result of the elimination of

jobs in this area. And we have not talked about the tragic reductions in the timber sale programs on the other National Forests in California, Washington and Oregon. The big picture shows that there is going to be a severe crunch in the entire Region because of the Owl. I believe it is time for you to say "NO" to the Audubon Society, as well as the rest of the "environmental faction." We, who live and work in the woods, are entitled to the same quality of life as people who live in the city. I sometimes think that the Public Officials who make decisions about natural resources are too influenced by these groups, thinking that they represent, or are in fact, the public. These "radicals" have nothing to lose. We have everything to lose, and I believe the "country folks" of the West are going to rally together, and may even come to your city "en-masse" to help you understand that we are fighting for our livelihood. The people of this community are angry, and they wish to enlist the aid of every political ally that they can to ensure their future.

Thank you for this opportunity to comment on a very sensitive issue.

Larrie W. Mason
Executive Director

Iron County   **Kane County**
Parowan, Utah   Kanab, Utah

Dear Mr. President,

ACCESS TO PUBLIC LANDS
Washington County, Utah recommends clear policy guidance to federal agencies that will clarify and define the rights of local governments to claim public rights of way under the provisions of Revised Statute 2477 (formerly codified at 43 CFR 932).

This statute allows local governments to use, maintain and improve public roads that cross federal lands and that existed prior to October 21, 1976.

WILDERNESS POLICY
       Washington County, Utah recommends that all future wilderness designations exclude areas containing resources necessary to the economic well-being of the affected local residents. Also, the management of designated wilderness areas must provide for the necessary public access to maintain resources including but not limited to water, minerals, timber, rangeland and intensive recreation uses.

SUSTAINED MULTIPLE USE PRINCIPLES
       Washington County, Utah is highly dependent upon federal lands, which comprise 75.8 percent of the county land base. It is essential that these federal lands be managed so as to allow appropriate multiple uses. Attempts by narrow interest groups and federal agencies to restrict land uses on federal lands should be reviewed and closely coordinated with affected local governments.

Dee G. Cowan   Vince Underwood
Commission Chairman   Commission Chairman
Iron County   Kane County

California Outdoor Recreation League, Inc.
Newberry Springs, California

Dear President Bush,

THE CALIFORNIA DESERT: ITS ECONOMIC WEALTH AND POTENTIAL IN JEOPARDY
       Take an instant to look around you. Every item for the sustenance of life comes from the earth, be it lumber, pulp for paper, minerals to manufacture our necessities, the metals for vehicles, oil and

gas for transportation and warmth for comfort, food for the table, and forage for livestock. The earth carries the aquifers for our water. Man must have access to, and use of the land for survival.

In 1907 the first National Forest Director, Gifford Pinchot, stated, "Conservation and wise use of our natural resources is the savior of mankind." In large part we are dependent upon the Federal Lands for these natural resources. The economy of the nation must rely on the wise use of such materials, yet over the last thirty years there has been a very small, but powerful segment of our population that is determined to restrict the use of the lands through a land use classification designated as Wilderness. With a big "W" wilderness lands may not be entered by any means except muscle power. No motorized nor wheeled equipment is permitted. Recently, bicycles powered by man's muscle have also been banned in numerous wildernesses.

Of the 762 million acres of federal lands in the USA, more than three million acres are closed to any productive use, either by this classification, or study for future inclusion. This is de facto wilderness. They are determined to close all of OUR PUBLIC LANDS.

Having learned this, our immediate interest lies in the fourteen million acres of federal lands in the eastern California Desert, most of which is in the proposed Mojave County. Mining, grazing, military use, and recreation is much of the economic base for the county. We must not allow this huge portion of federally managed land to be closed to a NO-USE concept. Yet the latest proposed legislation would do just that.

Early in January of 1988, Senator Alan Cranston re-introduced the California Desert Preservation Act, Senate Bill 7. Many people have worked diligently since to have the bill withdrawn. It is dead for this year. We can thank Senator Pete

Wilson for refusing to endorse S-7 in time to get action this session. However, Senator Cranston won't give up easily. In 1985 he introduced the bill under S 2061. He vows to bring a new bill early in 1989 and promises to ask for an increased amount of acreage, as has happened each congressional session since 1971.

The first bill was to create the California Desert Recreation Area, but recreation in their terms was restricted to hiking. In 1974, there were two bills to be more restrictive and to create a California State park, under State Parks Director William Penn Mott, Jr. The park would cover two million acres between I-15 and I-40, bordering on the Colorado River on the east and the Cady Mountains on the west. Many of us went to work then. By June, one of the bill's authors wrote to the promoter of the bill saying, "I am convinced you and Bill Mott are the only two people who support this bill. I have received over fifty letters expressing the most strenuous opposition to this measure, and even less confidence that all forms of outdoor recreation would be allowed." With that, the bill was deep-sixed; we had won that first one. A new tactic was soon to surface, and continues today.

(Note: William Penn Mott, Jr. is the present National Park Director, and does not make a decision without consulting the Sierra Club. We have a direct quote of his own on this.)

By 1973, Senator Cranston was carrying the Environmentalists' torch for as much federal land closure as possible. That year he introduced ten wilderness bills, all designed by the environmental activists to close public lands to any use except hiking. Oh yes, you could go hunting and fishing, but how for can you carry a deer? When an environmentalist stakes his claim on "multiple use" of wilderness, this is the use he means.

Next came a series of bills that would place

more than fifteen million acres of the then eighteen million acres in National Parks under the Wilderness Classification. A typical example is Yellowstone National Park. Of its 2,220,000 acres, less than 3% has ever been open to the public for other than hiking.

Today, the National Parks and Conservation Association says our national park system is too crowded and withering from lack of care, and in order to remedy the problem, they are asking for 86 new parks and additions to the existing ones as soon as possible. Additional acreage to Death Valley and Joshua Tree Monuments, plus two and a half million more acreage for the East Mojave National Park here in our area was contained in S-7. Does this make sense?

In 1976, Congress enacted the Multiple Use Act, saying they recognized the need for conservative use of our national resources, but that was short-lived. A new administration soon took over under President Carter, who took his directions from the small but powerful Group of Ten. Today, so many of its disciples are members of congress that it is difficult to get sensible legislation through. But we must unite and try.

We must strive to keep the desert open for productive uses. With modern methods of gold recovery, there are several mines in production and there is a growing need for gold in industry. Much gold is used in the manufacturing of aircraft, in the engines and in the windshield construction against icing.

There are at least forty-six known strategic minerals in this desert. Recently I was privileged to listen to U.S. Congressman Larry Craig of Idaho. He told us of the Platinum Group Metals. If we didn't have access to them, we would lose $3 billion dollars annually in our economy, in jobs and in our ability to keep air as clean as it currently is. He said,

"Because I'm talking about automobiles, I'm talking about catalytic converters that require platinum in the making, and I'm talking about access to it in the Republic of South Africa, from where we have been importing platinum until the recent sanctions. The cost of each automobile can easily be upped to $400 to $500. Do you know where we are getting our platinum now? From the Soviet Union; they have just opened another mine in the Ural Mountains. You say we don't have platinum in the United States. Well, I don't know that we do and there are a heck of a lot of good geologists that don't know either. We might have, but if we progressively continue to lock up the land under which it might rest, then we will never know. Like we now know in Nevada that we have a gold boom going that ten or twelve years ago if you asked, the U.S. Geology Survey would have said, 'to the best of our knowledge, no, lock the land up.' But now look at the gold bonanza at Gold Bar and the new mines going on line in northern Nevada."

The population that does not profit directly from the economics of the desert resources must become aware that true conservationists care about the lands, they use it for the benefit of mankind. Ecology is man's relation to the land, conservation is wise use of the land for mankind, and environmentalism is a movement unrelated to the needs of man. Let's discount the environmentalists!

Let us be vigilant, be ready to oppose next year's Mojave Desert Preservation bill. Support only those candidates who oppose closure of OUR PUBLIC LANDS. It is a known fact that the Group of Ten have their Wilderness Green Book Agenda in readiness for the next administration.

With permission from Ron Arnold, I offer the following:

A CIVILIZATION ETHIC

I pledge to help to produce, to wisely use, and to preserve the resources of my civilization, its food, fiber, minerals, energy, education, government, institutions, economic security, and ideals, and where possible to protect its wildlife and natural beauty. I will respect the earth's ability to support civilization, striving to minimize pollution and disruption of the natural world. I will respect the technical processes that are essential to the operation of civilization, knowing that they are as interdependent as any ecosystem. I will strive to recognize the benefits and limitations of civilization in relieving human misery, and in opening opportunities for a life of security, fulfillment and the refinements of aesthetic appreciation for its citizens.

-- from the book *Ecology Wars*

Hildamae Voght
Executive Secretary

Kaupanger Logging, Inc.
Burney, California

Dear President Bush,

Following are our recommendations to resource departments under the new administration:

RECOMMENDATION TO U.S. FOREST SERVICE AND THE B.L.M.

Situation: Wildlife biologists employed by the U.S. Forest Service have little or no understanding of wildlife management. This causes them to make their decisions regarding wildlife to be narrowed down to preservation only because they have little knowledge about management.

Recommendation: Establish a minimum requirement of wildlife management education for all wildlife biologists employed by U.S.F.S. and B.L.M.

RECOMMENDATION TO DEPT. OF INTERIOR AND THE U.S.F.S.
Situation: Unroaded areas on national forests immediately adjacent to wilderness and national parks are vulnerable to forest fires because we are allowing our wilderness and parks to burn up. We must try to protect our dwindling timber base from fire.
Recommendation: Where possible, establish passable fire lanes for fire fighting vehicles along the boundaries of the national parks and wilderness for containment. Where it is not yet economical to build roads, establish heliports to facilitate fire suppression. As a point of interest, the U.S. Army is in the process of phasing out the Vietnam War era Huey helicopter; what an excellent firefighting machine it would be!

RECOMMENDATION TO THE U.S.F.S. AND B.L.M.
Situation: In 1984, Congress decided where the wilderness boundaries should be. Much of the timberlands left open to wise use is unroaded and therefore vulnerable to forest fire.
Recommendation: Establish rudimentary access roads into unroaded national forests for basic emergency use such as fire suppression and search and rescue. Each road should be yearly maintained and locked up until such time as a wise use access road is built.

RECOMMENDATION TO THE NATIONAL PARK SERVICE
Situation: 1988 forest fires in national parks.
Recommendation: Eliminate the "let burn" policy. That each and every national park establish

a system whereby two park officials experienced in fire-fighting establish contact with pre-arranged local forest service and state firefighting officers immediately upon receiving word of fires within their park and use every means available to put it out.

David Kaupanger
President

Southern Oregon Resources Alliance
Grants Pass, Oregon

Dear President Bush,
    Southern Oregon Resources Alliance is a community-based citizen group which held its first meeting in January 1977. Prompted by Congressional wilderness bills relating to the Siskiyou National Forest, the group's original thrust - community education, and informed local participation in land use decisions - remains its primary purpose as a non-profit corporation. It is SORA's basic premise that *Man* as part of the environment depends on natural resources for economic independence and recreation. SORA believes that protection of the environment is essential and can be effectively combined with utilization and development of our resources to provide both jobs and recreational opportunities.
    In states such as Oregon, which is over 50% publicly owned -- some counties are as high as 90% in public ownership -- it is essential that local people be heard by decision makers as more and more pressure is applied for single uses -- wilderness, wildlife or botanical preserves, etc. -- at the expense of the eminently sensible and productive multiple use concept for public lands. Multiple use allows everyone a piece of the pie -- miners, hikers, timber

fallers, hunters, cattle grazers, picnic parties -- all of us are able to get what we need from the land yet leave it for other users as well.

In addition to the newsletter and regular monthly meetings, major activities will continue to include:

1. Widespread participation in both USFS and BLM planning processes, as well as state and local activity;

2. Washington watch: numerous trips to Washington D.C. and Salem, local appearances by Congressmen, White House Staff, Administration Appointees (EPA, CEQ, etc.), state agencies;

3. Workshops and conferences for interested citizens: detailed presentations about specific issues. For example in 1978 we did a 2 day session called "Man & The Environment: Is there Room for Us?" A follow-up session in 1987 was called: "Man and the Environment: The Owls are Ahead!" Other meetings have addressed spotted owls, wild & scenic river legislation, forest fire salvage, etc.;

4. Downtown business community involvement. Our board members are bankers, retailers, local government officials, superintendent of schools, miners, timber operators and retirees. Our offices are shared with the Chamber of Commerce and Rogue Community College so we have a strong *Community Base*;

5. Demonstrations when all else fails to reach our legislators! Most exciting example: The Silver Fire Round-Up - August 27, 1988. Over 1,300 log trucks from 6 states converged on Grants Pass for a show of solid support for salvaging the burned timber in the Siskiyou National Forest. *It is* being salvaged!

Ann Basker
Executive Director

Northwest Legal Foundation
A Public Interest Law Firm
Seattle, Washington

Dear President Bush,

The NORTHWEST LEGAL FOUNDATION is a nonprofit public interest law firm which handles only matters involving unlawful government action, excessive regulation and other abuses of power. We would like to use this opportunity to address three issues of concern to us: 1) government out of control; 2) unconstitutional "takings" of property without just compensation; and 3) the appointment of judges.

1. Government is Out of Control

When the Founding Fathers gave us a Constitution with a Bill of Rights, the underlying principle was *limited government*, to provide security against unnecessary and unreasonable government intervention in people's lives. There is no question that government today is out of control at all levels. This fact has a least three significant consequences.

First, there is virtually no accountability. The purpose of elections in a democracy is so that people have meaningful choices regarding who will represent them and how they will be governed. However, for various reasons, this accountability exists today only in theory, not in fact.

Incumbency has become a life-time job guarantee: with few exceptions, once you're in, it's for as long as you want the job. As one official has put it, what we really have is an "elected dictatorship."

Our organization was formed to help restore accountability in government. When government entities and officials act outside of their authority, we seek to hold them accountable for their unlawful infringements on constitutional and statutory rights.

Another significant fact is that *many people are simply too intimidated by their own government.* They fear reprisals, particularly those who by virtue of their job must continue to deal with government.

Second, there is far too much legislation. Legislators at all levels of government are churning out so many new laws and regulations so fast that not even the most diligent citizen could ever hope to keep up. This is due in large part to growing legislative staffs and the need perceived by legislators to do something "visible" to convince their constituents that they are worthy of being re-elected.

Legislation cannot make everything fair. It can't make everything just. It can't make everything safe. It can't make everything right.

Excessive legislation breeds contempt for the law.

Excessive regulation takes away from the people the power to make many decisions for themselves about their standard of living and priorities for spending their money. In the building and development industry, for example, local governments in particular seek to impose endless and increasingly expensive requirements for amenities that most people probably would choose not to buy if they had a choice.

Third, big government out of control is outrageously expensive. To try to cure every problem and every injustice is simply unrealistic. Excessive regulation is too expensive for government to enforce and too expensive for people to comply with.

2. There Is Too Much "Taking" of Property *Without Compensation, in Violation of the Constitution.*

Property rights are fundamental rights. Property consists not only in its ownership, but "'in the unrestricted right of use, en-

joyment and disposal. Anything which
destroys these elements of property, to
that extent destroys the property itself. The substantial value of property
lies in its use. If the right of use be
denied, the value of property is annihi-
lated and ownership is rendered a
barren right.'"

Ackerman v Port of Seattle, 55 Wn.2d 400, 409, 348
P.2d 664 (1960).

The 5th Amendment to the U. S. Constitution
guarantees that no person's property can be taken
for public use without just compensation. Yet one of
the increasingly recurring issues we see in our work
is unlawful takings of property under the guise of
the police power, without any compensation, through
regulations which totally deprive owners of the
right to develop their property at all. In their efforts
to churn out legislation, officials seek to justify any
and every kind of restriction and condition by unsubstantiated assertions of government interest,
with little or no regard for property rights of affected
owners.

Federal Executive Order 12630 entitled
"Government Actions and Interference With Constitutionally Protected Property Rights" signed by
President Reagan on March 15, 1988, in response to
a trio of U. S. Supreme Court cases affirming the
rights of property, is a significant step in helping to
ensure that at least the federal government does not
unlawfully infringe upon property rights. However, this order is meaningless unless it is property
and diligently enforced.

The "takings" problem is particularly acute
with regard to the "wetlands" issue, which is emerg-
ing as both a significant environmental issue and a
property rights issue. "Wetlands" are an absolute
nightmare for people who bought property for a dear
price with the intent to develop it.

The population is increasing, yet land use regulations such as those concerning wetlands significantly diminish the potential housing supply, which drives up prices -- all in the midst of a housing demand crisis!

Supporters of wetlands regulations justify them on the ground that wetlands are part of the ecological chain and that unrestrained development could have disastrous consequences that are yet unknown.   Current and proposed wetlands regulations go much too far in protecting against dangers that don't exist with respect to far more property than is necessary to accomplish whatever the real goal is -- all without compensation to the affected property owners who are forced to bear the entire direct burden that should more appropriately be the responsibility of the community as a whole. As one of our state supreme courts has stated:

> "...public officials...have no right or legitimate reason to attempt to spare the public the cost of improving the public condition by thrusting that expense upon an individual. [Citations omitted.] The greater the cost of accomplishing something which is considered to be in the public interest, the greater the reason why a single individual should not be required to bear that burden."

Burrows v. Keene. 432 A.2d 15, 20 (N.H. 1981).

With regard to wetlands, government needs to define what resources are really the object of protection and whether there is truly a need for it.

3. We Need Judges Who Affirm the Concept of Limited Governmental Authority to Interfere *With Constitutionally Protected Rights.*

The last issue which we would like to address

is the need for judges who truly affirm the concept of *limited governmental authority* to interfere with constitutionally protected rights. Too often, too many judges seem to have forgotten that constitutional rights are paramount and that government's power to interfere with those rights is limited and must be sufficiently justified. The combination of certain legal presumptions, burdens of proof, and undue deference to unsubstantiated legislative assertions, to name a few things, have resulted in erosion of constitutional rights by one of the very bodies whose purpose is to protect such rights.

In order to justify regulations under the police power, legislators are supposed to establish a legitimate governmental interest in regulating a certain matter. There must be a real harm or problem serious enough to warrant regulation and the regulation must actually serve the asserted governmental interest. Assertions as to the existence of sufficient justification are easy to make but not so easy to prove. However, numerous judicial decisions reflect a tendency on the part of many judges to accept unhesitatingly the mere unsubstantiated assertions of legislators regarding the justification for particular regulations. As our Washington State Supreme Court has stated: **"[T]here is sometimes a natural tendency on the part of the courts to stretch [the police] power in order to bridge over otherwise difficult situations, and for like reasons it is a power most likely to be abused."** *Conger v. Pierce County,* 116 Wash. 27, 198 Pac. 377 (1921).

As a result, social activist legislation in recent years has led courts to water down certain fundamental rights by upholding a variety of regulations which not only significantly infringe upon constitutionally protected rights, but also ultimately work to the detriment of the very people the regulations were intended to help.   Particularly with regard to the protection of property rights, concerning which our U. S. Supreme Court justices have said: "Our social system rests largely upon its sanctity, 'and that State or community which seeks to invade it will soon discover the error in the disaster which follows.'" *Block v. Hirsh*, 256 U.S. 135 at 165 (dissenting opinion of McKenna, J.: White, Ch.J. and others).

Although many of these issues arise in state courts, the federal courts can lead the way. This requires judges who believe that the "ends do not justify the means", and who will make the government carry its burden of adequately justifying the need for its laws within the limitations of their authority.

For instance, trying to help low-income tenants by imposing onerous fees, conditions and other exactions solely on owners of low-income property is not objectionable because of the ultimate objective, i.e., to help low-income people, but rather, it's objectionable because of the means chosen to achieve it. If the "ends" are allowed to "justify the means", then the law becomes meaningless. And the prospect of living in a society where law is uncertain or disregarded at will is totally contrary to our system of government and is a serious threat to its very foundation.

SUMMARY
We urge you to consider the following:
1. Help to bring government under control by:
a. seeking to **restore accountability**, such as measures that will enable more qualified people to run for elected office against incumbents and help to break the "incumbency for life" pattern;

b. **discouraging the proliferation of legislation** that is not absolutely necessary, and the need for large staffs that promote the vicious cycle of bigger government and more law-making; encouraging people to assume more responsibility for themselves while admonishing them that laws can't make everything fair, right or safe -- the laws are only as good as the people who are supposed to comply with them;

c. **eliminating excessive regulations and programs which are outrageously expensive,** turning over more responsibility to the private sector and to state and local governments where the people have more control over their elected officials and tax dollars can be more efficiently spent; making it safe and worthwhile for "whistle-blowers" to report excessive and wasteful government spending; and reducing programs and/or requirements which are not absolutely necessary -- compliance with which we can no longer afford.

2. *Prevent unlawful infringements on property rights by:*

a. vigorously enforcing Federal Executive Order 12630; and admonishing state governments to follow suit;

b. promoting a "wetlands" policy that:

i) defines the real resource to be protected; clearly establishes, by *objective criteria, that regulation is truly necessary to protect against known, existing dangers*, and that the object of the regulation is a legitimate interest of government;

ii) *significantly restricts the definition and criteria of property that will be regulated* (compared with existing definitions and criteria) in such a way as to minimize the total amount of property rendered undevelopable or otherwise useless, specifically excluding smaller parcels and avoiding criteria which would render undevelopable large areas of property based on a determination that only a very small area fits the criteria;

iii) *recognizes the occurrence of a "taking"* of property requiring just compensation to the extent property is rendered undevelopable as a result of being classified as wetlands;

iv) *recognizes that wetlands can be filled* and developed without substantial adverse effects.

v) *spends 99% of the efforts on 90% of the problem* rather than 90% or more of the efforts on 10% of the problem.

vi) *eliminates conflicting criteria and requirements* of multiple jurisdictions exercising authority which presently infect the permit process with impossible bureaucratic tie-ups.

3. *Appoint judges who:*

    a. don't legislate from the bench;

    b. believe in the supremacy of the Constitution and the

    concept of limited government; and

    c. do not allow the "ends" to justify the "means".

Sally Saxon
Attorney At Law
Of   Counsel

Montana PLUS
Public Lands Used Sensibly
Bozeman, Montana

Dear President Bush,

Montana PLUS is a non-partisan, non-profit Montana corporation organized to inform and educate the public about the importance of multiple-use management of our public lands. Bruce Vincent (Libby, MT) is president, Gary Langley (Helena, MT) is vice-president, and Barbara Kapinos (Bozeman, MR) is secretary/treasurer.

Through Montana PLUS, people representing hunters, snowmobilers, trail bike and ATV riders, rock collectors, mining, agriculture, forest products, oil and gas, handicapped and disabled people, water users, wool and stock growers, and others, are working together to define the issues regarding multiple use management of public lands.

Roughly one-third of Montana's land is federally owned, with no property tax revenues from them going to local governments, and approximately 3.8 million acres of that land is designated Wilderness. Combined with frivolous appeals of land management plans by self-appointed "environmentalists," and raging wildfires throughout 1988, the amount of Wilderness in Montana had come to be seen as a threat to jobs and highly valued recreational opportunities. This public sentiment led to President Ronald Reagan's veto of Wilderness legislation in November, 1988, and to the defeat of Sen. John Melcher by Conrad Burns in the general election of November 8, 1988, due to Sen. Melcher's "mishandling" of the Wilderness issue, according to the defeated senator himself.

Speakers at the organizational meeting of Montana PLUS in Bozeman on November 18, 1988 included U.S. Representative Ron Marlenee (R-MT); California State Senator H.L. "Bill" Richardson; Grant Gerber, Wilderness Research Impact Foundation; Charles Cushman, National Inholders Association; and Clark Collins, Blue Ribbon Coalition. All speakers emphasized that organizations and individuals concerned about the impact of additional lands being designated Wilderness must be organized and that a non-partisan public education and information program was vitally needed.

Working people needed to be become involved, the speakers said, because Wilderness designation prohibits development of resources which provide the jobs. Recreationists need to be involved, the group was told, because Wilderness advocates are anti-recreation, and only 4 percent of the American public ever use Wilderness areas for recreation.

With the defeat of the 1988 Montana Wilderness Bill, multiple-use advocates had won round one of a multi-round fight, it was agreed, and the need for further public education was identified. Funds were collected to hire a professional media production team to create broadcast and print advertising, and to produce a 30-minute video for television programming, and for distribution to grass-roots organizations throughout Montana.

Bob Garner and Ken Eurick, both Montana residents with extensive experience in media production, were contracted to do this job, the first television spots have been produced, and the 30-minute video production is underway.

Bibliography

NUMEROUS BOOKS EXPLAIN portions of the Wise Use Agenda, but as yet none can truly be regarded as comprehensive. The following list is offered in double service: first, to serve as source notes and background references for the recommendations in the Wise Use Agenda; second, as a general reading list for the intelligent layman on the subject of wise use of the environment.

Anderson, Terry L., editor, *Water Rights: Scarce Resource Allocation, Bureaucracy, and the Environment* Pacific Institute for Public Policy Research, San Francisco 1983

Arnold, Ron, *At the Eye of the Storm: James Watt and the Environmentalists* Regnery Gateway, Chicago 1982

Arnold, Ron, *Ecology Wars: Environmentalism As If People Mattered* Free Enterprise Press, Bellevue 1987

Barrons, Keith C., Ph.D., *Are Pesticides Really Necessary?* Regnery Gateway, Chicago 1981

Claus, George, and Bolander, Karen, *Ecological Sanity* David McKay, New York 1977

Committee for Salmon Enhancement, *Salmon Enhancement in Washington State,* Washington State Environment and Natural Resources Committee, Washington State Senate, Olympia, September 1988

Council on Environmental Quality, *Environmental Quality,* 17th Annual Report, U.S. Government Printing Office, Washington, D.C., 1988

Deacon, Robert T., and Johnson, M. Bruce, editors, *Forestlands: Public and Private* Ballinger Publishing Company, Cambridge, Massachusetts 1985

Florman, Samuel C. *The Existential Pleasures of Engineering* St. Martin's Press, New York 1976

Gabor, Dennis, *Innovations, Scientific, Technological and Social* Oxford University Press, Oxford 1970

Gughemetti, Joseph, and Wheeler, Eugene D., *The Taking* Hidden House Publications, Palo Alto, California 1981

Hall, Cameron P., *Technology and People* Judson Press, Valley Forge 1969

Heidegger, Martin, *The Question Concerning Technology* Harper & Row, New York 1977

Holmes, William H., *Forestry by Coercion* Holmes & Co., Forbestown, California 1983

Hummel, Don *Stealing the National Parks: The Destruction of Concessions and Public Access* Free Enterprise Press, Bellevue 1987

Hummel, Don, and Hummel, Eugenia *One Man's Life: From Wagon Wheels to the Space Age* Free Enterprise Press, Bellevue 1988

Keenan, Charles J., *Environmental Anarchy: The Insidious Destruction of Social Order* Cappis Press, Victoria, British Columbia 1984

Libecap, Gary D., *Locking Up The Range: Federal Land Controls and Grazing* Pacific Institute for Public Policy Research, San Francisco 1981

Lovelock, J. E., *Gaia: A New Look at Life on Earth* Oxford University Press, Oxford 1979

Lowrance, William W., *Of Acceptable Risk: Science and the Determination of Safety* William Kaufmann, Inc. Los Altos, California 1976

Machan, Tibor R., and Johnson, M. Bruce, *Rights and Regulation: Ethical, Political, and Economic Issues* Pacific Institute for Public Policy Research, San Francisco 1983

National Conference of State Legislatures, *A Legislator's Guide to Forest Resource Management* NCSL, Denver 1982

Ottoboni, M. Alice, Ph.D., *The Dose Makes The Poison: A Plain Language Guide to Toxicology* Vincente Books, Berkeley 1984

Paul, Ellen Frankel, *Property Rights and Eminent Domain* Transaction Books, New Brunswick 1987

President's Commission on Privatization, *Privatization: Toward More Effective Government,* U.S. Government Printing Office, Washington, D.C. March 1988

Schnidman, Frank, Abrams, Stanley D., and Delaney, John J., *Handling the Land Use Case* Little, Brown and Company, Boston 1984

Siu, R. G. H., *The Tao of Science: An Essay on Western Knowledge and Eastern Wisdom* The M.I.T. Press, Cambridge, Massachusetts 1957

Soderberg, K. A., and DuRette, Jackie *People of the Tongass: Alaska Forestry Under Attack* Free Enterprise Press, Bellevue, Washington 1988

Task Force on Outdoor Recreation Resources and Opportunities, *Outdoor Recreation In a Nation of Communities,* U.S. Government Printing Office, Washington, D.C. July 1988

U.S. Department of Agriculture, *Wilderness Management* by John Hendee, et al., Forest Service Miscellaneous Publication No. 1365, U.S. Got. Printing Office, Washington, D.C., 1977

Williams, Roy E., *Waste Production and Disposal in Mining, Milling, and Metallurgical Industries* Miller Freeman Publications, San Francisco 1975

Index of
The Wise Use Movement
Listed by State

The two hundred twenty-four citizen organizations, government agencies and individuals listed here attended or supported the Multiple Use Strategy Conference in August, 1988 at Reno, Nevada, where the Wise Use Movement mandated the publication of this agenda. The public interest organization participants in the Wise Use Movement represent memberships exceeding ten million Americans and Canadians. The Canadian contingent supports the U.S. Wise Use Movement's recommendations to President Bush to enhance cordial international relations, but submitted no recommendations of its own.

For those one hundred fourteen leaders of the movement that contributed statements, the page number of their statement is indicated after the name. The people of the movement are a resource themselves to be wisely used by all.

Idaho

Kentucky

New Mexico

Ohio

Ontario, Canada

Oregon

Virginia
Peggy D. Hart, Vienna
Constance Heckman, Arlington

Washington
Barbee Mill Company, Inc., Bonney Lake
Bremerton Cruisers, Bremerton, 43
Center for the Defense of Free Enterprise,
    Bellevue, 86-89
Columbia Gorge United, Stevenson
Committee to Preserve Property Rights, Cook
Eastern Washington Dirt Riders, Kennewick, 43
Iconix, Mill Creek
Lake Chelan Snowmobile Association, Chelan, 43
Lake Union Association, Seattle
Mr. and Mrs. John R. Lathrop,
    Bonney Lake, 59-60
National Association of Reversionary Property
    Owners, Issaquah, 121-122
National Park Users Association,
    Bellevue, 103-114
Northwest ATV Association, Monroe, 43
Northwest Independent Forest Manufacturers,
    Tacoma, 50-52
Northwest Legal Foundation, Seattle, 143-150
Pacific Northwest Four Wheel Drive Association,
    Longview, 43
Public Land Users' Society, Tacoma, 53-55
Ridgerunners ORV Club, Republic, 43
Roadrunners Motorcycle Club, Tacoma, 43
Skagit Motorcycle Club, Mount Vernon, 43

Tacoma Motorcycle Club, Puyallup, 43
Tree Farm Services, Hoquiam
Washington ATV Association, Enumclaw, 43
Washington Contract Loggers Association,
    Olympia
Washington Friends of Farms and Forests,
    Olympia

Washington State Snowmobile Association,
        Kirkland, 43
Western Forest Industries Association, Olympia
Wild Rivers Conservancy Federation, Forks
Yakima Valley Dust Dodgers, Yakima, 43

Wyoming
Casper Dirt Riders, Casper, 43
Citizens for Multiple Use, Dubois
The Dubois Alliance, Dubois
Lander Snowdrifters, Lander, 43
Outdoors Unlimited, Beulah
Sour Doughs Snowmobile Club, Lander, 43
Sweetwater County Snowpokes, Rock Springs, 43
Wind River Multiple Use Advocates, Riverton, 97
Wyoming State Snowmobile Association,
        Pinedale, 43
Wyoming Trail Machine Association, Story, 43

TELEGRAM FROM PRESIDENT BUSH

To a member organization of the Wise Use Movement:

```
TWX WHITEHOUSE
JANUARY 17 1989


NATIONAL CONFERENCE ON FEDERAL LANDS
LAS VEGAS, NEVADA

DEAR FRIENDS:


IT IS A PLEASURE TO SEND GREETINGS TO THE
NATIONAL CONFERENCE ON FEDERAL LANDS.  I
AM COMMITTED TO ENSURING PROPER STEWARD-
SHIP OF THE PUBLIC LANDS WHICH ARE SO
INTEGRAL TO LIVES AND LIVELIHOODS IN THE
WEST.  I COMMEND YOUR EFFORTS TO HELP
ADDRESS THE CHALLENGE OF MANAGING THESE
RESOURCES FOR THE BENEFIT OF ALL AMERI-
CANS.  WITH YOUR HELP, WE WILL MEET THAT
CHALLENGE.

SINCERELY,

GEORGE BUSH
```

QUANTITY DISCOUNTS
The Wise Use Agenda
Give a copy to everyone you know!

Now is the time to get this book in the hands of every American. Order 25, 50 or 100 copies. Send them to your friends. Give them to business associates. Mail one to everyone you know.

DISCOUNT SCHEDULE

1 copy	$9.95	25 copies	$175.00
5 copies	$45.00	50 copies	$300.00
10 copies	$85.00	100 copies	$500.00
	500 copies $2,000.00		

ORDER YOURS TODAY!

Merril Press
P.O. Box 1682
Bellevue, WA 98009

Please send me _____ copies of THE WISE USE AGENDA. Enclosed is a check or money order for $_____.

Please charge my ☐ VISA ☐ MASTERCARD

Number_____Exp. date_____

Signature_____

Name_____

Street_____

City_____

State_____ZIP_____

Phone (_____) _____

QUANTITY DISCOUNTS
The Wise Use Agenda
Give a copy to everyone you know!

Now is the time to get this book in the hands of every American. Order 25, 50 or 100 copies. Send them to your friends. Give them to business associates. Mail one to everyone you know.

DISCOUNT SCHEDULE

1 copy	$9.95	25 copies	$175.00
5 copies	$45.00	50 copies	$300.00
10 copies	$85.00	100 copies	$500.00
	500 copies $2,000.00		

ORDER YOURS TODAY!

Merril Press
P.O. Box 1682
Bellevue, WA 98009

Please send me _____ copies of THE WISE USE AGENDA. Enclosed is a check or money order for $_____.

Please charge my ☐ VISA ☐ MASTERCARD

Number_____Exp. date_____

Signature_____

Name_____

Street_____

City_____

State_____ZIP_____

Phone (_____) _____

QUANTITY DISCOUNTS
The Wise Use Agenda
Give a copy to everyone you know!

Now is the time to get this book in the hands of every American. Order 25, 50 or 100 copies. Send them to your friends. Give them to business associates. Mail one to everyone you know.

DISCOUNT SCHEDULE

1 copy	$9.95	25 copies	$175.00
5 copies	$45.00	50 copies	$300.00
10 copies	$85.00	100 copies	$500.00
	500 copies $2,000.00		

ORDER YOURS TODAY!

Merril Press
P.O. Box 1682
Bellevue, WA 98009

Please send me _____ copies of THE WISE USE AGENDA. Enclosed is a check or money order for $_____.

Please charge my ☐ VISA ☐ MASTERCARD

Number_____Exp. date_____

Signature_____

Name_____

Street_____

City_____

State_____ZIP_____

Phone (_____) _____

QUANTITY DISCOUNTS
The Wise Use Agenda
Give a copy to everyone you know!

Now is the time to get this book in the hands of every American. Order 25, 50 or 100 copies. Send them to your friends. Give them to business associates. Mail one to everyone you know.

DISCOUNT SCHEDULE

1 copy	$9.95	25 copies	$175.00
5 copies	$45.00	50 copies	$300.00
10 copies	$85.00	100 copies	$500.00
	500 copies $2,000.00		

ORDER YOURS TODAY!

Merril Press
P.O. Box 1682
Bellevue, WA 98009

Please send me _____ copies of THE WISE USE AGENDA. Enclosed is a check or money order for $_____.

Please charge my　　　☐ VISA ☐ MASTERCARD

Number_____Exp. date_____

Signature_____

Name_____

Street_____

City_____

State_____ZIP_____

Phone (_____) _____